Not Great Hopes
A Birmingham Boyhood

To all those who made these memories, the living and the departed, and for my granddaughter, Ella May Traves and any future grandchildren, who hopefully will inherit them.

Not Great Hopes
A Birmingham Boyhood

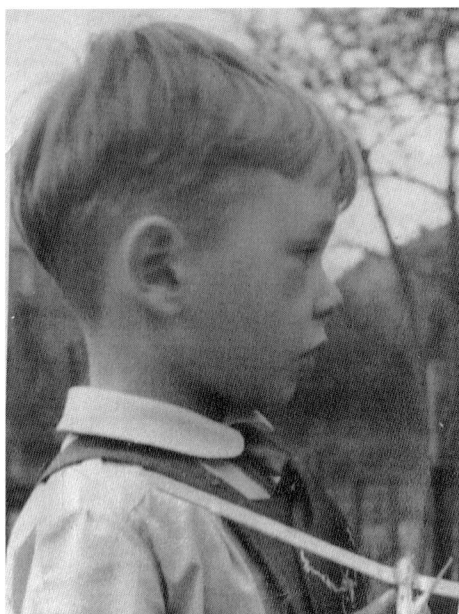

Peter Traves

BREWIN BOOKS

BREWIN BOOKS
56 Alcester Road,
Studley,
Warwickshire,
B80 7LG
www.brewinbooks.com

Published by Brewin Books, 2017

© Peter Traves, 2017

A CIP catalogue record for this book is available
from the British Library

ISBN 978-1-85858-563-5

Printed in Great Britain by
Hobbs The Printers Ltd.

Contents

"One has not great hopes from Birmingham. I always say there is something direful in the sound."
Emma by Jane Austen

Preface

I HAVE been much haunted by ghosts in recent years. Not ghosts of the white sheet or clanking chain variety but ghosts nevertheless, memories that evoke a dead past and, in many cases, dead people. These memories appear often unbidden and with great clarity. They bring back to life events, states of feeling and people with such force, such immediacy, that I seem for a moment to be back fifty or sixty years ago; to be once again that distant small child, that adolescent or young adult. They are evidence that the person I was still exists somewhere in my memory and, at the same time, they are a poignant reminder of the irretrievable loss of that self, those moments and those people in any form of external reality.

For years I thought about setting these experiences down in print. I felt that such an exercise would help me place those memories and that in struggling to find the right words I might, perhaps, find the right relationship to these past events and people. However, anyone who has tried to write will know how cunningly the mind procrastinates. There will always arise those hitherto unimportant tasks that suddenly take on a new urgency. There is always the prospect of a future time when there will be the space and the inspiration to begin work. Thus in this way I put off making a beginning and I have little doubt that these memories and reflections would have remained unwritten.

What then changed? What was the prompt that made me sit down and commit words to the page, or more accurately, to the screen? It was changed by several deaths and a birth. The deaths were of aunts and uncles. It was all too apparent that the generation of adults from my childhood was disappearing. Thinking of them brought a new sharpness and a new poignancy to the scattered memories of my childhood. The birth was of my first grandchild, Ella. She will, I hope, live well beyond me and well into the twenty-second century. Perhaps, I thought these memories if set down, might be of interest to her, might perhaps provide some insight into what will become increasingly an image of a very different era, another life. These memories may give some sense not only of her grandfather's life, but also of life as lived in an age more distant to her than the Victorians were to me in my childhood. And so I made a start.

Mum and Grandma Underhill on my first outing – Frome 1950.

This is not an autobiography, the subject for a start is too obscure for that, though it is wholly autobiographical. Nor is it a social history, lacking the objectivity or research for that, though it may cast light none-the-less on life as it was lived over half a century ago. It is rather a series of memories and reflections based on a boyhood spent in Birmingham and covers the period from 1950 to 1968 with a brief epilogue from the last few years. These memories are united by the association with a place, Birmingham. Part of the purpose of writing has been to try to understand the relationship that I have not only with the past, but also with the city of my childhood.

1

Life at Fairway

38 Fairway 2016.

AFTER THE Second World War my father served in Palestine with the 6th Airborne Division. Palestine had been a British Mandate since the end of the First World War but during the 1940s tensions had increased and Britain's attempts to curb Jewish immigration resulted in an outbreak of increasingly savage terrorist activity. The paratroopers played their part in quelling riots and in attempting to act as a buffer between the recently arrived Jewish immigrants, many of whom were holocaust survivors desperate for a homeland with security and the displaced Palestinians and their Arab supporters who felt a profound sense of betrayal that their interests were being ignored or sacrificed. It was a bloody and thankless task for the British forces and yet my dad looked back on this period of his life with genuine warmth. He often talked of the comradeship of his fellow troops and of the landscape, at once hostile and extraordinarily beautiful.

On his return he was stationed at Warminster in Wiltshire and my parents lived just over the county border in the tiny Somerset hamlet of East Woodlands. How-ever, my parents and their families came from Birmingham and it was to there they returned when my dad left the army in late 1953. I was nearly four years old at the time. He found a job with the Gas Board in Northfield but the real challenge was finding a place to live. The baby boom, bomb damage and the desire to clear the slums, had created huge pressure on available housing. My parents applied for a council house but the waiting list was depressingly long and they would have faced many years before any kind of ac-

Dad in army uniform
in Palestine.

commodation could have been available. So they moved in with my maternal grandparents, grandma and granddad Underhill.

Grandma and granddad lived in a terraced council house, 223 Cliff Rock Road in Rednal on the very southern edge of Birmingham. They had moved there from rented accommodation in Handsworth in the 1920s. In those days getting a council house usually meant a step up in terms of housing from what was on offer for working people in the private rented sector. Number 223 came with a fine view of the Lickey Hills though in later years the view was blocked by new flats built on Leach Green Lane. The house comprised a living/dining room, a good sized kitchen and pantry, a bathroom (a later addition to the original house), and three bedrooms. There was a back yard and a long though narrow garden behind the house and a reasonable sized front garden. Access to the front door was via a path shared with one set of neighbours and to the back door via a covered alley-way shared with the neighbours the other side. Those are the mere physical details of the house but it came to have for me an enormous emotional significance. It seemed to me to be the centre of the extended Underhill and Vincent families. It was where I felt most secure and most loved.

With three bedrooms there was space for my grandparents, my Auntie Joan, and the three of us. It may have been tight by modern standards but people expected to share rooms and there were many families in far more cramped and far more inadequate accommodation at the time. However, my parents, particularly my dad, wanted their own house and when my mother became pregnant again it made the matter more urgent. They tried once more to get on the council's housing list but again prospects were grim so they looked to buy with some help for a deposit from my grandparents. So it was that early in 1955 we moved to 38 Fairway.

Me, Richard (my brother) and Keith Jones (friend) in the track behind Fairway, July 1959.

Fairway was an inter-war development just off the Bristol Road South between Northfield and Longbridge. It was effectively a crescent that backed on one side onto a track that ran above Hanging Lane with the North Worcestershire Golf Club beyond and onto the open space of Green Park on the other. The houses were all pretty well identical, three bedroomed with one

11

being a very small box room. They had two small downstairs rooms with the front one being bay windowed and the rear having french windows that opened onto the garden. They had been built with upstairs bathrooms but outside toilets, though, as was the case with number 38, many had been connected to the main house by way of a lean-to shed or garage. The land rose behind with increasing steepness as you moved up the outer semi-circle of houses, the even numbered side. Thus, as you moved up the road so the gardens became increasingly steeply terraced. The people who lived in Fairway in the 1950s came from a mix of backgrounds and included a German professor at Birmingham University. However, the majority were from working class backgrounds with a significant proportion employed at the nearby Austin Motor Works.

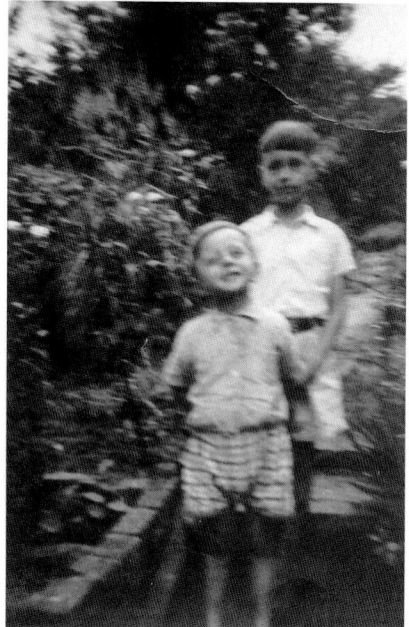

Me and Richard in the garden of 38 Fairway, 1958.

Number 38 was pebble-dashed, still very much in fashion at the time. You reached the front door up a short, steep drive with steps to one side. You entered a narrow hall that had been oak panelled as if this were some miniature Jacobean mansion. The kitchen at the end of the hall was tiny but there was a small larder. Out the back was a yard, then steps up to a small lawn and then a sloping set of flower beds, two apple trees and a few black-currant and gooseberry bushes. There was a gate at the top of the garden that opened onto the track that ran above Hanging Lane.

None of the houses in Fairway that I ever went into had central heating. In fact to have central heating, like having fitted carpets, was regarded by my parents at that time as a sign of great affluence or feckless expenditure. The house was heated by coal fires in the downstairs rooms. There had been fire places in the two larger bedrooms but these had been plastered over in a modernising move that pre-dated us. Modernising was very much the fashion of the 1950s and 60s and much promoted on TV programmes fronted by DIY experts like Barry Bucknell who could show you how with some plywood you could cover up those awful old panelled doors or how to get rid of the old fashioned stucco decorations on ceilings. The underlying aim was to eradicate original period features as quickly as possible and replace them with a smoother surfaced, and, as it was then seen, more sophisticated style. Ironically, those poor benighted, old fashioned souls who kept the original features, were able in later years to sell their houses at a markedly higher price when, and if, areas became gentrified.

So, no central heating and only coal fires in two downstairs rooms. This fact had serious implications for the way we lived, perhaps not at a profound or spiritual level, but certainly at a superficial and practical one. A coal fire has to be laid, lit and drawn. There is an art to laying a fire; not one I ever really mastered but I did have a rudimentary grasp. Whoever got home first in the winter was expected to lay the fire. First the ashes from the previous day had to be raked out from under the grate and safely deposited in what was then aptly named the dustbin. Then kindling wood and screwed up newspaper were laid as a base for the fire with small pieces of coal placed on top. The fire could then be lit. However, it had to be encouraged and this was called "drawing". In well organised households this was effected with a drawing tin, a metal sheet placed in front of the fire to direct the draught upwards, thus "drawing" the fire. Mum seemed to hold such an approach in contempt and chose instead to hold a sheet of newspaper in front of the fire. This worked well in terms of encouraging the draught and causing the fire to blaze. The gamble, however, was to do with timing. Paper is of course flammable. As the fire blazes up behind the paper so the paper heats and eventually catches fire. At this point my mother would skilfully push the paper up the chimney with a poker where it would be swept up and out by the strong upward draught. If it went wrong, as it did from time to time, it meant a blazing newspaper in front of the hearth. On one occasion it also meant a chimney fire. However, it made for excitement.

Once the fire was established it had to be kept in. It had to be fed just enough coal to keep it going but not too much to stifle it. On very cold nights, in order to keep at least some heat for longer, tactics were used to slow down the burn of the fire. Slack was added. Slack was fine low quality coal often rather damp and it produced a great deal of smoke and a minimum of heat. Mum added to this potato and other vegetable peelings. Occasionally this meant a fire of some kind was still burning in the morning.

Whether it was the design or the inefficient way in which we used it, the coal fire, though cheery to look at, was not effective in heating the house. We normally had a fire only in the rear living room. The chimney gave some warmth to the bedroom above that was shared by my brother and me, but few other places in the house benefited. Even in the living room the fire's impact was limited: too close to the fire and your legs were singed, more than a few feet away and the effect was minimal. As a result chairs tended to be grouped, not as now around a TV or in an open plan style, but around the fireplace.

On a cold winter's night moving away from the fire and out of the room was a chilling experience. The toilet needed a small oil lamp hung below the cistern to stop the pipes from freezing. There were occasions when the brick walls of our toilet were coated in ice. It certainly discouraged unnecessary or prolonged visits to the loo. Going up to bed meant rapidly taking off one set of clothes and getting into pyjamas as fast as possible before diving under the sheets, layers of blankets, the eiderdown and possibly heavy coats. Duvets were unheard of in my family. A hot water bottle was pretty well a necessity. Later in the mid-sixties the decadent luxury of electric blankets was a family indulgence. On particularly frosty nights ice would form on the inside of the bedroom windows and our breath would be visible in the cold air. Occasionally a paraffin heater was lit in the bedroom an hour or so before we went up to bed. These were relatively effective but potentially dangerous. Horribly scarred children bore witness to the dangers of paraffin heater accidents.

There was also the ritual of toasting bread before the fire. A pile of toast would be built up and periodically taken into the kitchen where my mother would coat it with pork or beef dripping with a sprinkle of salt. These would be eaten hot alongside the fire as more bread was toasted. No doubt this meal was not good for us, layers of pure meat fat building up in our veins, but it was wonderful. The dripping was rich in meat flavour and before the coal fire we became greasy of hand and mouth as we worked our way through the pile of toast.

Although we had no central heating there were two sources of energy to heat water. The first was a back boiler to the fire. This was used throughout the colder months when a fire was lit. At other times we had to use the immersion heater. The switch for this was located on the landing outside the bathroom. When it was turned on a red light illuminated a small disk that rotated at alarming speed to indicate the amount of electricity being consumed. The fire provided a relatively cheap but limited supply of hot water while the immersion heater provided plenty of hot water but was very expensive. As a consequence we had to be careful about using hot water. Showers were not common, in fact no one I knew had one. Washing was something that you did on a daily basis over a sink and in the weekly bath. Bath night in our house was Sunday. Mum and dad had their baths in the late afternoon. My brother Richard and I shared a bath just before bedtime. Being the oldest I had the luxury of the deep end. We were allowed a short period of play in the bath and then mum would come up to give us a good scrubbing with a large red block of Lifebuoy Soap. This soap, later reserved for heavy duty clothes washing, was pretty coarse stuff and there were numerous times when it brought my skin out in a stinging red reaction. Luxury soaps like Camay and Lux were items reserved for better off or less prudent families. Shampoo did not feature at this period in our house; the Lifebuoy did for body and hair.

For much of the time we lived at Fairway most of the furniture was second-hand, acquired largely from relatives. Like fitted carpets and central heating, a matching three piece suite was a positively upmarket item in houses of the 1950s and early 60s and suites regularly featured as the star prize on quiz shows. We had, therefore, in the living room a motley assortment of chairs and a rug on a lino floor. Lino was commonplace as the cheap option for floor covering. Bare floorboards in working class homes were likely to be a sign of poverty rather than a nascent taste for a later middle-class life-style feature. Upstairs furniture was sparse. Again the beds, at first, were second-hand with metal frames.

For several years we had no television and the main source of entertainment was the radio. This sat in a corner of the room. Radios at this time were generally large items set in a wooden or bakelite frame. They used valves rather than transistors and consequently took a long time to warm up so that the sound gradually built and coalesced into meaningful language from the hums and disparate fragments of the competing frequencies of the different stations. Then there was the process of tuning the radio in. A dial on the front of the radio indicated the probable, or at least possible, location of a particular station. So around the dial were written what seemed to me exotic and distant locations such as Berlin, Luxemburg or Rome as well as the BBC Light Programme, the BBC Home Service and the BBC Third Programme. Announcers on all BBC channels still spoke with cut glass accents.

"This is the BBC Home Service. Here is the news..." with each word sharply differentiated.

At my grandparents *The Archers* was an established tradition at just after 7pm each evening however this was not adopted at Fairway. My principle memory is of Sunday morning and afternoon. Around lunchtime it was *The Billy Cotton Band Show* with the popular band leader raucously opening it with his cry, "Wakey wake-aaaaaay!"

followed by a top speed rendition of his signature tune, *Somebody Stole My Girl*. The show was a mixture of comedy and live music with singers Alan Breeze and Kathi Kay and the pianist, later to be a star in his own right, Russ Conway. Apparently, or so one website claims, Michael Palin and Terry Jones wrote jokes for this show!

Each week we tuned in around the main meal time to *Family Favourites* hosted by Cliff Mitchelmore and his wife, Jean Metcalfe. This was a record request programme designed to connect servicemen stationed abroad with their families at home.

"This is a request from Private David Roberts stationed at BFPO 40 for his wife Angela and their children, son Michael and daughter Pauline. He says he is missing you all and that it won't be long until Christmas 1959 when he returns home. So Angela, here for you is Vera Lynn singing *It's a lovely day tomorrow...*"

It was not until many years later that I realised that BFPO stood for, British Forces Posted Overseas. BFPO 40 was, I think, West Germany, where Britain had a large military presence at the time. What did strike me even then was the length of separation that was often alluded to in that restrained style of the day whereby Christmas 1959 might be eighteen months away; eighteen months of further separation and strain for these families. At Christmas time there was an extended programme and contact was made with more distant postings in Singapore, Hong Kong or Aden. Contact was dependent on making the radio connection and this was not always successful or sustained.

"Aden can you hear me? This is London. Come in Aden."

Each week the most requested record would be designated the "Bumper Bundle". It was often a title that held a poignant reference to separation and the longing for reunion. Anne Shelton's *Sailor* was a popular choice with lyrics that must have struck a strong chord with many separated families.

"All my love is there beside you...Come home to me."

Also on a Sunday was the *Navy Lark* with the famously incompetent crew and then the wonderful *Round the Horne* with its glittering cast that included Kenneth Horne, Hugh Paddick, Betty Marsden, Bill Pertwee and Kenneth Williams. Regular characters included Rambling Syd Rumpo, a folk singer played by Kenneth Williams where virtually every line of every song was some kind of thinly veiled sexual innuendo. A celebrated event was ye olde English tradition of Formation Goat Nadgering. I still remember many of the sketches from this programme including one that was a pastiche of the popular prisoner of war escape stories in which two characters are anxiously discussing recent bungled escape attempts including;

– And what about Smithers?

– Smithers? Ah yes, the plan to pole-vault over the wire.

– Well...?

– Ah...alas...poor squeaky.

Later in the afternoon from 1962, when it moved from its former Saturday setting, was *Pick of the Pops* hosted at this time by Alan Freeman who opened each week with;

– Hi there pop-pickers!

This was said as the driving signature tune pounded out in what I then took to be a mid-Atlantic accent. It was in fact his natural Australian accent. Such was my Brummie cosmopolitan sophistication at that time.

My parents were not mad about this programme, my dad describing most pop songs as, "a flaming row".

– Can you make out a thing they are saying Beryl?

– No Reg, I've no idea.

– Why can't they sing properly? Like proper singers.

Added to this was the decadence of male singers and groups who wore their hair "over their collars".

– A few months of National Service is what they need.

However they generally gave way and let me listen. The weekly singles charts were announced on this programme with the countdown from number forty to ten with all the new entries or major movers up the charts being played. Then the whole top 10 was played. It was a widely believed story that Alan Freeman talked over the introduction of each song in order to spoil any illicit recording that might be made at home.

Late afternoon, as a penance to mortify my ears as I saw it, mum insisted on listening to *Sing Something Simple* with the Cliff Adams singers, introduced each week with;

"Sing something simple

As cares go by."

I had to admit when pressed by dad that you could indeed hear all the words.

In later years we had a car and on Sundays, dad's only day off work, we often went for a drive into the country. We took trips out to North Worcestershire and the Vale of Evesham or even on occasions, Shropshire. I rarely looked forward to these trips as it often meant missing *Pick of the Pops*. I was allowed by the mid-60s to bring along a transistor radio which occasionally picked up a signal if I was very lucky.

A feature of shopping that was commonplace then, which faded for a while but has now come back with internet services and supermarket delivery, was the number of trades that called at the door. We, like most others, had our milk delivered daily. We used Midlands Counties Dairies, others used the Co-op. A bread van came several times a week. Coal was delivered from a cart pulled by a horse. The coalman was always in a blackened state and hauled one hundred weight sacks on his back through the lean-to and into the coal store in our yard. We also had soft drinks, pop, delivered to the door on a weekly basis by Corona. Butchers would, if asked, deliver meat to the door, usually brought by a young lad on a specially adapted bike of the kind seen in *Open All Hours*. Other tradesmen such as fishmongers and green grocers made regular visits to the road where they served from the back of the van. Periodically the rag and bone man with his horse and cart came up the road to collect unwanted goods.

Mum loved shopping in Birmingham town centre and this is where she tended to get most of her clothes. For me and my brother it was generally Foster Brothers in Northfield, harshly referred to in later years by fashion conscious school mates, as "Pantomime House". Shoes were from Clarks or Bata, again in the village. Supermarkets had not really arrived yet, although some local grocers brought in the exciting innovation of self-service. Sweets and drinks could be got from the Off-Licence. Behind the house was the track and down the track was a small single storey shop that served a wide range of groceries with lovely ham that was sliced on a machine with a lethal looking blade expertly handled by the assistant.

Northfield centre 1950s.

We were only at Fairway for twelve or so years. I have since lived in many places and in my present home for more than twice the time I lived at number 38. And yet, it still feels to me like the family home. It is the place I grew up in. If I was happiest at 223 Cliff Rock Road with my grandparents, I was at home in Fairway. It was here that many of the seminal experiences of my childhood took place. It was here that I grew from a pre-school child to an adolescent on the brink

Fairway 2016.

of adulthood. It was here that the drama of my parents' disintegrating marriage played out. It is here that most of the events and patterns that constitute for me in memory the essence of childhood are located.

2

And so to school: Part 1 – Primary School

– But I don't want to go to school.
I want to stay here with you.

– You have to go to school. If you don't go they
will come and take mummy and daddy away
and put them in prison.

THUS, IN early September 1955, my tearful protestations were overcome by mum's dire warning of the legal consequences of non-compliance with the 1944 Education Act. I decided on the spot that I was not prepared to push matters this far and duly trekked off to school.

I am a child of the post-war baby boom. There was as a consequence of this baby bulge a shortage of schools and Birmingham City Council embarked on a large-scale programme of school building in the early and mid-1950s.

A few months after moving to Fairway my brother Richard was born and that September, in 1955, I started school. New schools were being built in the area but they were not yet ready so I started at Tinkers Farm, an all-through school from Reception through to the last year in secondary, 15 in those days. The Reception department was not with the main school but comprised a temporary set of classrooms beside the entrance to Green Park on Frankley Beeches Road.

I have no real memories of Reception but I do know that I was allowed to walk to and from school at the start and end of the day and for lunch. The school was close to home, perhaps half a mile away and involved no crossing of roads but modern parents would probably be horrified at the idea of a child of five walking to and from school unaccompanied. This freedom, or parental recklessness, depending on your point of view, was for me a feature of my childhood and one that I think was of great benefit.

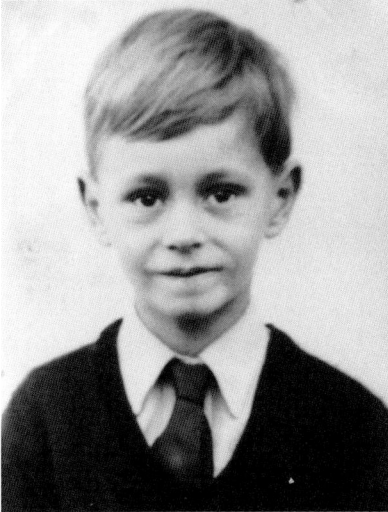

Me circa 1957.

After Reception I moved across to the main Tinkers Farm primary school site. This was a building dating from the inter-war years. There was a long corridor which ran outside the classrooms and adjoined the large playground. I have no memories of any lessons although I do recall that we had wooden handled pens with steel nibs which were dipped into an inkwell set into the desk.

While lessons are a blank to me now, I do have a vivid memory of belonging to one of the two gangs in my year. These were led by Kevin Cavanagh and Raymond Harborne. Everyone belonged nominally to one gang or the other. My membership was very nominal indeed. I was approached one day early on in the playground by Kevin's henchmen to ask if I would join his gang. It seemed like an offer I could not refuse. Kevin and Raymond were both what my mother would have referred to as "rough boys". They liked fighting and took the blows and bruises that came with it with admirable equanimity. I did not like fighting and regarded the avoidance of unnecessary pain inflicted by tougher and stronger boys as a major priority. Fortunately, though not gifted with physical strength I was gifted with an ability to run reasonably quickly and for a considerable distance. This generally sufficed to get me out of most scrapes.

At the time I was at Tinkers Farm we did not have a television. However, I was well aware that the great hit with boys of the moment was the American series, *Davy Crockett*. The tune that accompanied the show was a major hit and everyone of us knew the words.

"Born on a mountain top in Tennessee...Kilt him a b'ar when he was only three."

I had no idea at the time what was involved in "kilt him a b'ar" but I knew it was impressive whatever it was at three.

Popular also was the nylon imitation of the beaverskin hat that Davy Crockett wore. These were on sale in many toy stores and most of my friends and classmates had one. I did not. Ownership of such a hat was the essential passport to joining in Davy Crockett games at playtime. My mother resisted my pleas. She was not prepared to shell out the probably extortionate price demanded for this item even if such a refusal led, as I claimed, to my total social isolation and the dangers of long-term psychological damage and deflated self-esteem. I did not use that language of course but that was broadly the line of my whining attack on the brutal and uncaring attitude displayed by my mother on this issue;

– But mum, everyone has one.

– Not everyone, Peter. Your friend John hasn't got one.

– Nearly everyone.

– That's not everyone is it?

– It's nearly everyone and it means I can't join in the games.

– Why not?

– Because they won't let you without a hat.

– I don't think that's very kind. I wouldn't want to play with boys who were unkind like that.

Eventually one lunchtime mum offered a compromise. She would not buy one but she would make one. I was able therefore to go back to school that afternoon with the claim that I would soon be in possession of a Davy Crockett hat and therefore be eligible to join the break-time Davy Crockett games.

Mum found some old fur from a coat of an aged aunt. She then made it into a hat. She had used as the model an illustration from a book on Daniel Boone that I was reading. Now this particular illustration showed one of the early American frontiersmen, a hunter of the Crockett type, with a fur hat. A fur hat with two tails. This was therefore historically authentic and meant I had twice the tails on my hat of any other boy. Unfortunately the Davy Crockett hat shown in the series and copied in the imitation hats on sale in shops and worn by classmates had only one tail. Thus in their view I did not have one additional and bonus tail, but one tail too many. I never therefore gained full membership of the Davy Crockett group. Mum tried to console me by suggesting that the other boys had inferior hats that lacked both authentic material and design. I was not consoled.

Bellfield Infants and Junior Schools in Northfield opened by the time I was in the last year of Infants, 1957, and we all moved across from Tinkers Farm. The school was brand new. All the equipment was in pristine condition and the hall had that peculiar smell of a new building. I don't recall the name of our teacher in what was then top infants, Year 2 in new money. I remember that she was young or appeared so to us. Of the lessons I can bring to mind only two experiences: my first memory of being read to and my first experience of being smacked in school.

A hot afternoon. I was sleepy but entranced by the teacher's reading of the end of Robin Hood. Robin is dying. From his bed he summons his old friend Little John and his wife, Maid Marian. He fires an arrow through the window saying that he is to be buried where it lands. That is all I remember. I have no idea which book version this was from or who wrote it. All I remember is the sheer pleasure of listening to a well read story. It is a pleasure I retain to this day.

It is another warm day. It is afternoon again. We have been set work to do and the teacher leaves the room. Before doing so she tells us that anyone talking or making a noise while she is away will be punished severely. She will know who it is, she tells us, and we believe her. We are quiet for a while but she is absent for a prolonged period and gradually we begin to chat. More and more of us join in, more and more noisily. The teacher returns. She is clearly very angry. Whether or not she has been told off for leaving her class I don't know, but she is very annoyed.

– Right, own up all those who spoke while I was out of the class! I know who you are.

Now I had had it drummed into me that owning up to wrong doing was not only right but generally led to a much lower level of punishment and even at times to grudging praise and admiration on the part of the judge. Furthermore, she had told us she knew who had spoken so it would be wise to throw myself on her mercy through open admission of guilt. I put my hand up along with a girl, an equally misguided soul.

– You two out here now. Stand straight and take down those socks.

She then took a ruler and gave me and the girl several sharp blows on the back of the legs. Even at the time in my childish way I felt that this was not only unjust, she must have been aware that large numbers chatted in her absence, but also singularly stupid. The chances of anyone owning up to a misdeed in future had been all but eliminated by her action. The lesson for me was that owning up was an occupation reserved for the gullible and the weak minded. It was not a mistake I was likely to repeat, at least not in her class.

My first love happened at Bellfield and the subject of my affections was a girl in the top Juniors, Joyce Musgrove. Already popular with boys of her own age and some from the local senior school who hung about for her at the end of the day. Joyce, however, along with her friends, was clearly saving herself for the Everley Brothers who they worshipped and whose songs they practised endlessly in the playground. At this stage I was in the first year of Juniors, and she was way beyond my reach. However, one play time while being teased by a group of boys about my obvious crush my existence and my adoration were brought to her attention by her friends. Joyce and her group took pity on me and she hugged me and held me close to her for the rest of the break. For her it was an act of pity or a response to a very little boy as she would have seen me. For me it was heaven and it fuelled my dreams and my affection for the remaining months before she moved on to secondary school. It was not an event, I need hardly say, that was ever repeated.

Dad worked at the time at the Gas Board on the corner of Lockwood Road, in Northfield, just around the corner from school. He had only a brief lunch break and so it was imperative that I didn't dawdle on my way out to meet him at the school gate where he would wait with his aged, repainted and much repaired bike of monstrous size or so it appeared to me. On meeting me he would hoist me up onto the crossbar and we would cycle the mile or so home for our main meal of the day. I loved the sound the wheels made beneath me as they skimmed over the tarmac roads. The journey home was mainly downhill but the reverse was of course true on the return trip. The bike had no gears and yet I never remember being in the least aware of any strain on the part of my father.

In 1958 Meadows Primary School was opened. This would be our local primary and the expectation of my parents was that I would transfer there on its first day. Whether or not they registered me I have no idea but on the morning of the new term my best friend at Bellfield, John Thomas, called for me and mum clearly had a change of mind and I set off to my old school. However, this reprieve did not last long. For whatever reason it was decided that I would transfer at the end of that term. This was despite the pleas of the Bellfield Junior head teacher who assured my parents that I was on track to do well. I suspect looking back and based on the odd scraps of information my mother gave me in later years that my parents thought Meadows a more genteel school with fewer "rough children".

I owed a lot to Bellfield. The teachers there must have given me some confidence in my ability to learn because I left with a real passion for history. It was also the high point of my not very distinguished acting career, taking the lead in the Infant School play and the pinnacle of my public career being chosen to present flowers to Mrs Attlee, the wife of the ex-Prime Minister Clem Attlee, on their attendance at the official opening of the school.

So a new school and new classmates. The unfamiliarity was accentuated by the fact that at Bellfield we had been taught the Marian Richards handwriting style, whereas at Meadows they favoured the older copperplate style. The failure to fully readjust is reflected still in a hand that is an odd and largely unsatisfactory amalgam of the two styles.

At Bellfield and through books my parents had bought me I had gained a love of history. Here was a chance to shine in the new school. One day early in my time at Meadows the teacher asked;

– Where did the Normans come from?

Now the obvious and safe answer is, of course, Normandy, or perhaps, France. But I knew the Normans had settled in Normandy as Viking raiders from Scandinavia. So that was the answer I gave. I waited for the anticipated praise for the more sophisticated level of historical understanding this demonstrated.

– No. Where did the Normans come from? Can someone in class help Peter out on this?

Several hands shot up and one of the "good" girls answered with a look of supreme smugness and some contempt;

– France, sir.

I was mortified. In trying to be extra clever I had given the impression that I had not even the most basic knowledge of this the most famous event in our history.

The sensible move at this point would have been to have let it drop and shown my interest and knowledge over a longer period of time. I did not, however, take the sensible route. I said nothing at the time but appeared at the teacher's elbow the next day with my history book and pointed out the veracity of what I had said. I did this quietly but in full sight of the class. This was not a smart move.

Teachers rarely like to be corrected in this way and I must have appeared, as I probably was, a precocious and irritating brat. Generously he told the class that the point I had made was a good one. However, I feel it did not endear me to him and while at the time the epithet he used on many later occasions, "our resident historical expert" seemed to me a badge of honour, it later occurred to me as one perhaps laced with at least a touch of irony.

The first head teacher at the Meadows was Mr Walker, known to my parents as "Harry Walker". This familiarity had nothing to do with genuine acquaintance but with the fact that as Harry Walker, the head teacher also worked for the BBC as a swimming commentator. He was often away from the school presumably on commentating duty. Modern head teachers, with the enormous workload and responsibility they carry, would look with amazement now at a colleague trying to do two jobs in this way.

I cannot recall all the staff but a few stand out. Mr Williams was my class teacher for the first two or so years. He appeared to me relatively ancient but I suspect he was in fact no older than forty at the most. He was a strict but kindly man and we all liked him enormously. Mr Owen replaced Mr Williams in my final year. He was another Welshman but appeared to me a much more distant person than his predecessor.

Mr Summers was the handsome young teacher adored by the girls and admired by a number of the mothers. For their part the fathers were somewhat taken by the young Miss Stafford. Mothers tended to agree that, while "very nice", Miss Stafford's skirts were a "little tight" and she seemed a little too conscious of her figure. This was an early lesson in the fact that the judgements you make depend where you are coming from.

Out of the mouths of babes and sucklings comes unexpected wisdom sometimes providing a sharp insight that will last a lifetime. One afternoon in craft, a subject I neither liked nor did well at, someone in our group began talking about a local lad whose mother had cancer and was dying. I said how horrible it must be to know that each day is bringing you closer to death. Another girl in the group looked at me and said;

– But that's true for us all. Each day brings us nearer to death.

It was a reflection that stunned me at the time and looking back it was a bold thing for her to have thought and said, a kind of childish female Thomas Hardy, looking life's tragic fate fully in the face at the age of ten.

I was by this time a voracious reader. What I read was not shaped by parental guidance or even by the guidance of teachers. In the main, lots of history and whichever novels for children caught my fancy. I have always been a great re-reader, returning again and again to the books I most enjoy. This was a habit established early. At Meadows the book I re-read most was...well actually, I cannot remember the title and google has been no help in finding it. The central character was a wolf. No, it is not *Call of the Wild* or *White Fang* or any other book by Jack London. It is told from the point of view of the wolf and relates his life from birth to his leadership of the pack and on to his eventual death defending the pack from hunters. I was utterly engrossed by this story and read it again and again. If, as you will see later, Unstead's *History of Britain* sparked a love of narrative in general and of historical narrative in particular, it was this lost novel that planted a love of fiction.

Virtually every boy in my class admired Carolyn Pegg. She was mature beyond her years and very pretty. She was much fancied by older boys where she lived and probably regarded all of us as rather callow and immature. She showed no interest whatsoever in me except on one very perplexing but wonderful evening. It was towards the end of the final term and there was some kind of open evening and I was on duty as one of the librarians to show parents around. Carolyn was my partner for this task. As the evening wore on fewer and fewer parents made their way across to us and we began to amuse ourselves playing dare, truth, kiss or promise. At some point in this game Carolyn refused whatever absurdly silly dare I had given her but said instead she would give me something as long as I promised to give it back. She made me promise this solemnly. At this point she slipped off her chair opposite me and came across and gave me a long kiss on the lips. She then demanded the repayment. What this was all about I have no idea. I can only assume that the fumes from the book bindings had gone to her head. Nor did I have the time to build on this promising move as we left the school a week or so later.

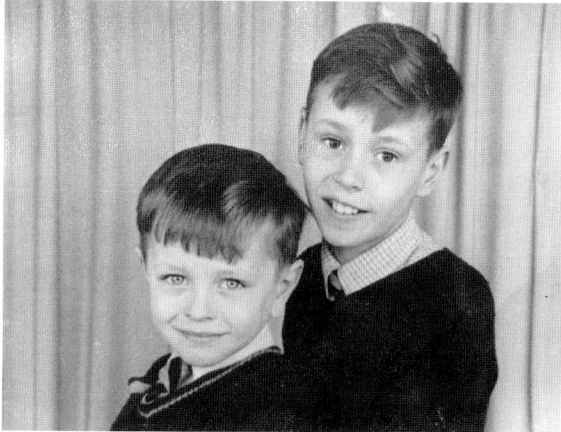

Meadows School photo – Me and Richard circa 1960.

In the 1950s, primary schools, particularly in the final two years were principally concerned with preparing pupils for the eleven-plus exam. There were regular tests and in the last year we were divided into two classes, the one in which the pupils were expected to pass and the one where they were not expected to pass the crucial test that would play such a huge role in determining our future lives. We even sat in the order in which we came in the major practice tests.

People talk nostalgically about a "grammar school system". This is a misnomer. It was a "secondary modern system". Most children went to secondary moderns and while there were many good secondary modern schools and a great number of dedicated and talented teachers in them, the expectations and outcomes for most children who went to them were very modest indeed. Even the much vaunted grammar schools produced a level of failure that would be unacceptable in modern schools with a small proportion dropping out at 15 with no qualifications, a larger proportion dropping out at 16 after 'O' levels and only a tiny minority going onto university. Nevertheless, a place at grammar school was seen as a vital stepping stone to later success. Failure for those with any chance of passing was regarded as catastrophic.

I do not remember much about the exam itself, save sitting at my desk waiting to start. Of the content of the test I have absolutely no recall. Then having taken the exam there was the long wait for the result. Birmingham sent out all the letters on the same day and that morning I was cleaning my shoes on the steps outside the kitchen when the postman arrived. Mum was clearly in a state of considerable anxiety. The issue was not only whether had I passed the test but had I passed it well enough to go to my first choice, King Edward's Five Ways. I think, though I cannot be certain, that the letter was handed to me for opening. What is certain is that I was still outside on the steps when the news was announced either by me or one of my parents that I would indeed be going to Five Ways.

Then it was off to school to share the good news with the others. I usually travelled in with the Sargent twins, Noel and Sybil. Sybil was not in the top class and was not expected to pass. Noel was and thus the expectation was that he would be going on to grammar school. He had not passed. His devastation was all too evident as he was comforted first by his parents and then the gentle and kindly Sybil. It certainly took the gloss off my triumph and was the first inkling for me that this was neither a sensible or a humane way to educate children.

Leaving the Meadows, and the last day in particular, was the first great parting of the ways for me. I had left Bellfield it is true but that was an individual thing with no preparation or ceremony. Here it was different. We had been together for three years. We all knew each other and there were tight friendship groups in the year. You grow and change a lot at that age and we had done that growing and changing together. Now we were to be scattered across numerous schools and there would be some people who I had seen most days for three years who I would never see again. Such occasions have always stimulated the strong streak of sentimentality in my nature and conjure up a melancholia that is relatively gentle but quite profound. We collected autographs, writing in the books either messages of deep friendship or attempts at great humour. I seem to recall I simply signed my name being unable to think of anything clever or moving to say. One girl, Lynda Smith, a pretty girl, wrote in my autograph book the enigmatic line, "The cause of many a silent tear". For months after I reflected on this deeply romantic statement of a passion she had obviously kept secret and only revealed as we were to part. It was over a year later that I noticed the corner of the page was turned over and on it was written, "The Answer". Turning it back I read, "An onion". Disappointed as my vanity was, I could at least console myself that I had not made a deeply embarrassing response in the light of my original misreading.

The years up to the end of primary school seem in memory to occupy a disproportionate amount of my life with each succeeding phase representing an ever truncated period of time. Perhaps it is the fact that six years in the life of an eleven year old is a very big proportion of the life lived so far. Perhaps it is the degree of change that takes place between 5 and 11 which is greater by far than changes made in any subsequent six years. Whatever the reason it still stands out as a long and generally very happy period of my life. I was secure in primary school and had established my place within it. Both Bellfield and Meadows were caring and happy schools and I certainly benefited from this. I formed close friendships though significantly they did not survive the move to secondary.

Perhaps the archetypal memory of these years is as follows. It is a bright already warm morning in early summer and the sky is clear blue. I walk, or more likely run to school in some imaginary role, perhaps as a knight or as a cattle driving cowboy. I might meet friends on the way. I arrive and we gather beneath the trees at the end of the playground to share our experiences of the evening before, to talk of some TV episode, or to plan what games to play at break time.

Meadows Primary School Football Team 1960-61.
Mr Summers the admired teacher and Paul Mallinder as
captain. Me fourth from right back row.

My home life seems secure even if we do live a bit in the shadow of my father's occasional dark moods. I have yet to understand the implications of these moods or of the cloud that is growing over my parents' relationship. I have friends, and while not the leading boy in the school or my circle, I am reasonably popular. I am a fairly large fish in a very small pond. All seems well. The change of schools would rapidly bring not only a dramatic change to my school life and my status therein, but also sadly, to my perception of just how insecure the happiness my home life really was.

3

The Book

ONE LATE Autumn or Winter's day, I cannot be sure which, I went into Town with my mother. Town meant only one thing to us – the centre of Birmingham. It was only later that I understood it as a generic term. To this day it still retains this dual meaning for me.

Mum regarded these trips as a source of great pleasure. I did not. They started early in the morning and lasted typically until late afternoon. We traveled there by bus and then spent hours looking around shops – Lewis's, Grey's, Henry's and, purely out of interest, the rather exclusive Marshall and Snelgrove's. Rackham's came later and marked a frisson of metropolitan excitement through its association with Harrods of London. Little would be bought and sometimes nothing. The pleasure for my mother was simply in window-shopping. Her energy on these trips was extraordinary and the pace unrelenting. Occasionally we stopped for a brief cup of tea at one of the department stores. We might or might not stop for lunch and in later years this could mean, as an act of real sophistication, a salad at the Ceylon Tea Centre. But in between it was remorseless. Each floor of each store was visited. Every item in sales trays examined.

By mid-afternoon I was invariably tired, bored and increasingly petulant. Mum regarded this behaviour with disappointment and as a mild form of an unfilial attitude, a kind of betrayal. The trips always ended at the bus stop in Navigation Street where we might, on odd occasions, have a baked potato or a bag of chestnuts. But what marks this particular day out is the book.

My first memory of pleasure from reading. I must have been around 6 or perhaps 7 years old. At some point on what was a cold, damp and increasingly foggy day we went into Midland Educational Books on New Street. The shop has long gone. The book I chose was *From Cavemen to Vikings* by R.J. Unstead. It was the first volume of Unstead's children's history of Britain. Later I was to get the whole text in one hardback volume from my Aunt Joan. This first volume was thin, with a woven cloth cover. It was illustrated with relatively simple black and white drawings that I found hugely evocative.

We boarded a number 61 bus and took seats upstairs. This had the advantage for me that standing was not allowed on the upper tier. The expectation in those days was that any man would give up his seat for a woman, and a child for any adult. The disadvantage, though scarcely noticed as it was so familiar in that period, was the fug of smoke. Passive smoking was not a recognised concern in the 1950s.

I began to read as we headed out of Birmingham, along Bristol Street past the Horse Fair and the Bristol Cinema where I was to see a number of great epics as a boy, onto the Bristol Road through leafy Edgbaston and past King Edward's High School. Past the University Tower, from which my best friend Paul Mallinder's grandfather fell when it was being built and survived with only a broken leg. Up through Selly Oak past the newsagents belonging to the family of Jessie Lilley, the friend largely estranged from my mother since her marriage to my father. Onto Bristol Road South and the tree-lined dual carriageway. Past the pond at Bournville. Up through the centre of Northfield, the "Village" to distinguish it as a shopping centre from the "Town". Then right at The Black Horse onto Frankley Beeches Road where soon after we got off at Hanging Lane.

Outside the street and shop lights were blurred by the increasing density of the smog. Inside I entered into the world of early Britain. Unstead may not be a great historian, or, for all I know, even a good historian. But my debt to him is infinitely greater than to all the much more distinguished historians I read later. It is greater also than the debt I owe to all the great writers of fiction I would come to revere. For he laid down a lifelong passion: for narrative in book form, for reading in general and for reading history in particular. In this book, simplistic and inaccurate as it probably was, I first felt that thrill of entering another age, imagined the experiences of people who lived generations ago and felt the engagement of a story in the relating of history.

One particular image stayed with me. It is an illustration. A column of Roman soldiers are marching out from a stone fort. At the head of the column is a mounted officer. The accompanying text tells of the return of the Romans to defend their Italian homeland from barbarian invasion. Hopelessly inaccurate it may be. Simplistic, undoubtedly, and yet nothing before had so caught my imagination or so successfully brought alive the sense of an age coming to an end. It is not an exaggeration to say that I was touched by this. Not in the sense of moved to tears but in the sense that I enjoyed an emotional engagement with a text; was imaginatively connected in some way to an experience of real people dead over a thousand years before I was born.

Almost fifty years later I was reminded of the intensity of this experience when reading a new translation of the great and ancient epic *Gilgamesh*. The narrator, writing down a story over three thousand years ago that must have been around for at least a thousand years before that in oral form, tells of the hero's fear of death. The fear is so wonderfully realised that we are reconnected with this man across the millennia. We hear his voice and remarkably we recognise our shared mortality and our shared humanity: the common ground of our experience.

Unstead's book, my mother's gift, bought perhaps to pacify a tired and resentful child, is my first memory of such an experience. It was the first link in a long chain of such experiences; the foundation of a key pleasure and a vital component of my life. I have never before attempted to express my gratitude to them both, the author and my mother, for this precious gift. These few inadequate words are such an attempt.

4

Holidays

– Only six more weeks and we go away

MUM'S statement, made out of the blue as we sat at the table one summer evening gave me a thrill of excitement. It was now real. Weeks not months. For a child weeks are just about imaginable as units of time. Six weeks – a space of time to be counted down. We took our holidays late – last week in August and first week in September. "Best time of the year" according to my parents and I accepted this judgement unquestioningly until well into my twenties.

Though money was scarce and, as mum later told me, some months they wondered where the mortgage payment of £10 would come from, my parents managed somehow or other, to take us on holiday most years. They were often cobbled together at the last minute, my father perhaps borrowing a van in which we would travel and sleep, or borrowing an old tent and hiring a car. All this, the cost, the organisation, the negotiations, took place for me behind the scenes and meant nothing. In fact I was entirely unaware of the effort involved but for me the holiday was the highlight of the year.

One year in particular I remember vividly. The night before we set out dad and I went to collect the car we were to hire. Mum and my brother Richard waited at my grandparents in Rednal while we walked the mile or so down to Rubery. The car's owner lived in a modest suburban house in a quiet road just off the village centre.

The car was ready for us in the garage drive. Dad paid and we climbed into a bullet nosed dark green Ford Prefect. I sat in front, a great treat for me, for the short drive up to my grandparents. Then all four of us drove home to Fairway.

Dad believed that long journeys should be started early, well before sunrise. To this day driving late at night or early in the morning before light retains an element of excitement and anticipation for me. Richard and I were sent to bed early. Pointless in many ways as I was far too excited to sleep until deep into the night. Sometime round about three or four in the morning I was wakened and urged to dress quietly so as not to rouse my brother who was carried sleeping into the car. In memory my summer outfit was always a red pullover with the folded collar, khaki shorts, a two coloured elastic belt with a snake fastener and Clark's sandals. Voices were hushed and when I did speak it seemed unnaturally loud against the still night. Half dazed I waited while the car was packed. Then my brother and I were sat in the back of the car, clothes and luggage placed around us and a tartan travel rug pulled over us.

Richard snuggled up and went straight back to sleep. For me there was no such possibility. I was impatient to be gone and irritated with my parents with their packing and checking and worst of all their insistence on a cup of tea before starting. At last they climbed into the car and we were off. Out down Fairway, right onto West Park Avenue, left onto Hanging Lane, onto Tessall Lane and then at the George pub crossing the Bristol Road South onto the south bound carriageway. On past the Longbridge factory, out through Rubery and beyond the City limits into the country.

The Bristol Road South was our local main road that ran past my Primary School, the location for our local shops and the route to my grandparents and to Town. It was, however, also the great A38, that major trunk road that led to the south-west, to Somerset, Devon and Cornwall. We followed this road for a large part of our journey as our holidays were invariably in the south-west, from Dorset across to Cornwall. So out through Rubery to Bromsgrove, Bromsgrove to Droitwich, Droitwich to Worcester, Tewkesbury, Gloucester and Bristol. In those days, before motorways and bypasses, long journeys were marked by villages and towns. Motorways have undoubtedly improved travel times, when they are free from traffic jams and roadworks that is, and have saved towns from the worst of through traffic. However, on a motorway progress is marked not by arrival at villages and towns but by huge blue signs telling where you could turn off for those villages and towns. Like air travel, it is motion without much sense of travel. By contrast in the fifties the journey took you through places. It was punctuated by the familiar townscapes, often seen deserted in the dark of the early hours or awaking as we traveled further south.

The journey was long, and we did not arrive until well into the afternoon. Cars were slower and there were few dual carriageways. Sixty miles an hour felt positively reckless and to average much over thirty meant good progress. As a consequence we needed to stop a number of times on the way. For me these stops were a distraction, an interruption to the pleasure of travel, something to be suffered as a necessary evil. As dawn broke we pulled in at the side of the road. My parents started up the primus stove and boiled a kettle for tea and cooked bacon and eggs for our breakfast. Such sights common in those days are rare enough today to attract attention as an eccentricity. The first break was probably in Gloucestershire, north of Bristol. A second was in Somerset, north Dorset or north Devon, depending on the destination.

As we journeyed there was a sense of growing expectation and even concern in my parents' conversation about the approaching challenge of Porlock. I knew of this hill long before I heard of the man from Porlock who broke the rhythm of Coleridge's composition of *Kubla Khan*. The great question was, would the car make it up the hill?

– We're heavily loaded so it will be touch and go won't it Reg?

– We should be alright she's running nicely. I checked the radiator last night and we have water if she boils over.

Then we reached the hill. Along the roadside as we climbed in low gear, a series of casualties with bonnets raised from steaming engines. At last at the top my father relaxed and putting the car into neutral coasted down the other side to cool the engine. Thirty years later I approached Porlock in an early model of the Ford Escort with some trepidation only to find the car swept up the hill. Modern cars climb this hill with even greater, almost contemptuous ease.

By early afternoon conversation turned to the first sight of the sea. Today for most of us holidays, while greatly enjoyable, are almost a commonplace. Many of us take several in a year and foreign travel is a norm not an exception. You have, therefore, to remember that in those years holidays were still great occasions and ordinary families could not afford more than a few days at a popular resort; many could afford nothing at all. Furthermore, Birmingham is one of the few great cities of Britain that is far from the sea. London, Glasgow, Bristol and Liverpool are ports on estuaries and a few miles from the sea. Newcastle, Manchester and Edinburgh are within a short drive of the coast. But Birmingham is almost a hundred miles inland. You have to appreciate what this meant. The sea was something I saw only once a year for a week or at most two. When the holiday ended it would not be revisited for twelve months, a lifetime for a child. The sea therefore occupied a place in my imagination as a child that it cannot occupy ever again. I was quite simply entranced by it and the most marvellous moment each year was the first sight of the sea. As we climbed hills we wondered would its brow offer that first view. Not yet. Then at last, far in the distance, blue, grey or green, sometimes silvered by the sun, the sea. Few moments in my childhood were so magical to me: few memories evoke such a poignant sense of loss.

Being on the beach was everything to me on holiday, that is what holidays were for. Everything else was a distraction. Waking up on holiday to rain meant other activities had to be planned. Perhaps a trip to a local town to shop or a visit to a castle. All day I scanned the grey sky for a chink of light, a glimpse of blue that might give hope. Once on the beach it was straight in the sea. One year we stayed in a wooden chalet above Widemouth Bay near Bude. This meant only a short walk down to this magnificent beach with its wide yellow sands. On each of the sunny days I stayed in the sea until I was blue with cold. Dad would come in with me, lifting me over the waves as they broke over us. Then at last, forced to come out I shivered as I was wrapped in a towel, waiting for the sun to warm me again.

Me at Land's End, September 1957.

Me climbing again! Widemouth Bay, Devon circa 1960.

Sandcastle building was supplemented at times by the creation of a sand car in which I sat and drove with a bucket steering wheel and spade gear stick. One year I decided, for some obscure reason to dig as deep a hole in the sand as I could. Deeper and deeper I went until the rim was well above my head. More and more excited by my accomplishment I drove the sharp edge of the spade deep into the moist, packed sand. I felt the sharp pain as the spade cut into my big toe. To my horror blood seeped up through the sand and my cries led to my rescue by dad.

This was not the only kind of rescue he had to undertake on this holiday. Cliffs were a source of great attraction for me. That attraction led, despite numerous warnings, to climbing. On many occasions I climbed beyond my ability or nerve and clinging to the rock face I had to call out to be helped down.

– How many times do you have to be told? Next time you can make your own way down.

A number of holidays in the mid-fifties were spent at Weymouth. I say a number because I don't know how many and sadly there is no longer anyone with whom I could check. In my memory it seems as if Weymouth was a constant in early childhood when I was an only child before my brother Richard's birth. In the albums I took from mum's house after her death there are a number of tiny black and white prints of my parents, singly, together, with me, with Uncle Les and Auntie Hilda or other relatives, on the sands or on the promenade of this Dorset resort. One picture moves me greatly. We are paddling facing inland. Clearly from our clothes it is a warm day. Mum is young, dark haired and pretty, in shorts and a bikini style top. Dad, tall lean,

Me and mum.

Me and dad.

Auntie Hilda, dad and mum,
Weymouth 1953.

moustached and handsome, in rolled-up trousers, an open shirt with turned-up sleeves. I am between them, about three years old, in dark woollen trunks. They are holding my hands looking down at me. My parents are now dead yet in this photo there is a record of them as they were: young and, perhaps, still hopeful, happy before the darker times when their marriage turned sour, and of me, secure before I had any sense of their natural, human imperfections.

Dad, mum and me, Weymouth 1953.

5

Cricket Practice

I WAS NOT a good footballer. At least such talents as I believed I had were not recognised by others and looking back they were entirely justified in this non-recognition. In particular they were not recognised by Mr Williams who picked the school team. I was an occasional player but never a regular team member. I was too timid in the tackle to earn a place as a defender. I lacked the control and decisiveness of a forward. Although a strong runner over a long distance, I did not have great pace over the sprint and the heavy, ankle chafing boots of those days, hard-toe-capped and stiff, were too much for my skinny legs. Cricket was a different case.

I had the advantage of considerable practice. Most of it was solitary and much of it without a ball as I mimed my way to huge scores in the back-yard. By playing outside the French windows of the living room I hoped to tempt my father out to play with me. However he worked six long days each week and it was therefore a real treat when he would appear out in the yard to bowl at me.

Occasionally we'd travel by Midland Red, more expensive but somehow more glamorous than the yellow and blue Birmingham bus fleet, across to my Uncle Geoff's in Solihull. In his living room there was a cup awarded to G. Traves as the best bowler in the 1958 and 1959 seasons. His garden was large by our standards, backing onto the monastery. Every visit I waited impatiently until they were persuaded to go out into the garden for cricket. Their own rivalry meant that the game was always a bit of a disappointment with few second chances awarded when I was out. Still it was all practice and all helped at the end of the day. I learned at least the right strokes and how to bowl over-arm with reasonable consistency and some pace.

I was not a great player but I had enough skill and know-how to hold down a regular place from the time I arrived at the Meadows. The Meadows Primary School was new in 1958. In its first year it had no top year, the oldest class was made up of 8 and 9 year olds. Our cricket team therefore found itself competing in the summer of 1959 against more established schools which could draw on 11 year olds. This did not seem a problem to us as we set out on the number 62 bus up to Rednal and across to Cofton Park for our first game. A sizeable group of parents came to watch. We were neat in our white shorts and shirts. The idea of defeat did not enter our heads.

Colmore Farm were our opponents. We arrived early and practised. Lightly bowling balls to each other. Many still bowling under-arm. Then we saw our opponents crossing the park towards us. Giants! At 11 they appeared almost men to us. Rougher than most of us as well. Our hearts sank and we had lost before one ball was bowled.

They won the toss and scored some unremembered large total. I had one moment of glory in throwing down the stumps to run one of them out. One of only about four wickets in total. Our turn to bat.

The pads were way too big for most us and there was little purchase on our bare legs. The openers walked out. A huge lad took the ball and strode back to the end of his run. He tore in and the ball shot past the batsman and straight into the mouth of their wicket keeper who lost both front teeth. Blood all over the place. We looked on in horror. We wore no boxes, helmets were non-existent in those days, no thigh or arm protection and thin rubber studded gloves. We were lambs to the slaughter.

I was not down to bat until number 7 but within three overs I was hurrying out to the wicket with my one pad, leading leg only.

Gloves were handed on from the player who looked all too relieved to be out and off I went. My tactics were simple but effective. Avoid any contact whatsoever with the ball by stepping rapidly across towards leg as it was released. It was remarkably effective and as I walked back to the oak tree that operated as our pavilion I left the bowler on a hat-trick. Nevertheless, my match had been a moderate success in my eyes given that I contributed one of our few brighter moments with the run-out.

We lost every game that season and by a big margin in each case. Two summers later it was a very different story. How much smaller 11 year olds had become by then. We were the same age as our opponents but we were battle hardened by two years of matches. We came into the season full of confidence. What we needed was practice. Evenings could be catered for by Mr Summers. However, this would not be enough and what was required was a weekend practice.

The nearby Green Park had few flat areas. It sloped steeply down the hill from Northfield village. The cricket practice for Meadows Primary School took place on one of the few level spaces, just big enough for a narrow pitch with the fielders spread out on the surrounding slopes. We had borrowed the heavy leather school cricket bag for the weekend. Dad had offered to train the team.

Dad at that time was in his early thirties. He was tall, well over six foot and slim. He wore a short cropped moustache and had fair slightly wavy hair brylcreamed lightly and pushed back. He was a fine sportsman: strong, quick and fearless. I was only ever quick. I feared him in some ways. He had a bad temper and was not averse to giving me a good hiding though he was not cruel or abusive in any way. Hitting children was not questioned in those days. However, I also admired him enormously. I knew that I was not physically strong or brave in the way that he was. I longed for his affection and praise. They were not easily or often given.

He organised the carrying of the bag across the park and selected the area for practice. It was clear from the start that my class-mates warmed to him. He said little but there was a strong sense of his authority. His easy ability to demonstrate the skills of batting, bowling and fielding impressed the team. He was also scrupulously fair showing me no favour whatsoever. I would not get to bat or bowl early, if at all in the final practice game. This was much appreciated by the others. I could see its point but regretted its consequences.

This Sunday morning was a culminating triumph for me. Others had said their fathers would take practice, but only my father had delivered on the offer. My occasional boasts along with all the others about what my father could do would be seen to be justified. As the bowler ran in I looked across at my father with the most profound admiration. This athletic and authoritative man who was impressing all my team mates was my dad. The ball struck me hard in the mouth, compressing my lip and splitting it. The shock was total. The pain was intense but subsided rapidly into a dull ache. No lost teeth, no lasting damage.

– If you'd been paying attention to the game instead of daydreaming it wouldn't have happened.

That was all he said. No words of sympathy, no words of concern. And they all laughed at this. It was at that point the tears came. Not from the pain of the blow but from humiliation and more particularly a sense of the unjustness of it all. I had not been paying attention because I had been staring in admiration at him. I had been looking away from the game, away from what should have been the prime focus of my attention to admire my dad. It was a looking away that was part of a deep desire for his admiration and his approval. I have sometimes felt that I spent a lifetime looking away in this manner.

6

East Woodlands

*– It looks like a nice day today. What about
a trip down to East Woodlands?*

A SUNDAY morning and this is how to the delight of mum and me, dad would announce a three hour trip down to Somerset every so often. It never once occurred to me at the time that there might have been prior discussion. Perhaps it had been planned and awaited only propitious weather. Perhaps it really was as spontaneous as it appeared.

I was a city boy, the son of at least two generations from Birmingham on my father's side and at least four on my mother's. But though city bred, I was not city born.

While dad was serving in the army in 1950 in Wiltshire my parents rented rooms in the town of Frome in Somerset and it was in hospital there that I was born in April of that year. Soon after they settled for the first four years of my life in a small cottage in the village of East Woodlands. While living at East Woodlands they, and in particular mum, had formed a close friendship with our neighbours the Lewers. Hence, these occasional visits to Somerset.

*Dad, mum and me 16 East
Woodlands, 1951.*

I described East Woodlands as a village earlier but it was little more than a hamlet in reality. Most of the properties and farms either belonged, or had until recently belonged, to the nearby Longleat Estate and the Marquis of Bath. The road from Frome to Longleat dropped down into the village and crossed a small brook before climbing sharply again towards the entrance to the estate less than a mile away. Near to the brook was a pub, the *Horse and Groom*. Its landlord, Mr Francis, ran the pub and the small farm

Granddad Traves, mum and me 16 East Woodlands 1951.

attached. Such arrangements rarely exist today. Across the stream and to the right of the road, were two small cottages belonging to the estate and enclosed by a stout hedge on three sides. To the side of the cottages a path shaded by trees ran beside the brook and wound round the outside of a field to the little church half a mile away on the edge of the great woods of Longleat. Opposite this path a narrow tarmaced lane ran for a few hundred yards with three or four thatched cottages beside it. It ended at a gate and beyond that a track ran to one of the larger local farms.

We had lived in one of the small labourers' cottages near the stream, 16 East Woodlands. Mr and Mrs Lewer and their family lived in the cottage attached to ours, 15 East Woodlands. It was this address with which I came to form such a strong emotional attachment.

The cottage had a single room downstairs, though a tiny kitchen had been subdivided from it. All the cooking in fact was still done on the living room fire and in the oven that adjoined it. Upstairs was reached through a latch door up a narrow staircase. The single upper chamber had been sub-divided with wooden partitions that did not reach up to the ceiling. In this cottage Mrs Lewer had raised five children.

There was in those days no inside water supply. Instead there was a standpipe shared with the neighbours out on the cobbled path that

Mrs Lewer – circa 1950.

ran in front of the two cottages. The toilet was around the back; a tiny room in which there was a planked seat with a hole in it. The contents of the basin below were periodically emptied at the bottom of the garden.

Having welcomed us Mrs Lewer would commence cooking. Meals at East Woodlands were on a gargantuan scale. My father and I, both big eaters, were invariably amazed by the quantities being prepared and cooked. Having filled a large enamel bucket with potatoes, Mrs Lewer would anxiously wonder whether or not this would be enough. Our unspoken view was that it would have sufficed for a week.

After the meal, weather permitting, it was over the stile into the large field next to the cottage where a game of cricket was played. I was always eager to show my sophisticated skills as a bowler but usually lost out to the more rustic but highly destructive batting of Vion and his grown-up brother Trevor.

As a small child what I remember are the visits at week-ends or on the return route from holidays. These lasted only a matter of hours but were much treasured. Later from about the age of ten I was allowed to stay there for a week or more by myself.

When staying I was allocated one of the spaces upstairs. Beside the bed was a pile of war comics, all based on the Second World War. They were full of heroic adventures by clean-cut British heroes, blond haired and with features that would, ironically, have made them ideal for SS Aryan breeding programmes. The Nazis by contrast were cruel and sneering but ultimately cowardly. The dialogue of the villains included phrases such as "English pig-dog" and an occasional example of a foreign language with the expression, "Donner und Blitzen!" The perfidious Germans were always ultimately outwitted by the guile, courage and sheer fighting ability of the Tommies. I loved them.

Me aged one, East Woodlands.

Cricket in the field next to the Lewers – me batting, dad wicket-keeper, Richard facing the wrong way!

Despite its small size there appeared to be no shortage of children between ten and sixteen in and around the village. Vion, some four or five years older than me and the subject of my hero-worship, would periodically choose or be cajoled by his mother into taking me out to join local youngsters at play perhaps over in the barn of a local farm. I came to suspect in later years that Vion's interest in some of the older girls had more than a taint of the carnal about it and I thus provided a useful cover story at times.

One hot morning, Vion and I, wandered across the field to the local church. We were accompanied by Brian Francis the son of the inn-keeper and Vion's closest friend. Brian, a heavy, good natured, slowly spoken lad was not given to abstract speculation but on that morning he opened to me one of my first experiences of what profound loss might be. We were seated on the grass in the churchyard. We were next to a gravestone, shining in its newness with clear golden lettering. I had taken little notice of it.

– He were just turned twenty-one were our David. I couldna wanted a better brother. I miss him every day and t'aint fair.

Looking up I saw tears in Brian's eyes and an expression of the deepest concern and care on Vion's face.

I learned later from Vion that David had been everything Brian was not: slim, athletic and outgoing. Brian had worshipped him as had his father and mother. About the age of nineteen he had gone to the doctors with a mild but persistent complaint. It turned out to be a fatal and incurable illness that was hereditary in nature. He died soon after his twenty-first birthday. Brian was to die of it some years later, also aged twenty-one. His father took heavily to drink and his mother was broken in spirit. The graves of all of them are now in the churchyard. Their inscriptions give only dates and such phrases as "Much loved son..." Behind these words is a village tragedy.

There is a misplaced photograph. I am eleven or so. Wearing borrowed swimming trunks, several sizes too big and held up with a belt, I am goofy, gangly and terribly skinny. It is a day at a local river with Vion and Trevor. It is a perhaps unflattering and inelegant record of that day, but it is a record nonetheless of a golden time.

For me as a child and adolescent East Woodlands *was* the English countryside. When people talked of the country for me that could only refer to East Woodlands. It inspired in me a deep love of an English landscape that is gentle, that has been shaped by centuries of human activity and which is typified by small fields, hedgerows, rolling hills and tiny villages. It is not of course the only English landscape. It is the English countryside of the south Midlands and the South West, and not even the whole of that area. There are other more dramatic landscapes in England but this is the one I came to love the most. Those much longed for trips and stays in East Woodlands came in later years to inform not only my affection for rural England but my enjoyment of the poets Thomas Hardy and Edward Thomas. When Thomas was asked why he chose to fight in the First World War being neither a hater of Germany or a strong nationalist in any sense at all, he simply picked up a handful of earth and said it was for this. I cannot claim anything like that level of passion or poetic affiliation with the soil of England, but having travelled and seen spectacular and breathtakingly beautiful scenery I know more than ever that no other landscape fills me with such a profound sense of belonging and affection. East Woodlands still stands for me as my first and defining view of rural England.

7

The Freedom to Roam

"If you don't stop it you're not going out to play"

WITH THESE words mum exercised her most effective deterrent for bad behaviour. Not going out to play entailed real loss as far as I was concerned and a similar strategy, employed equally effectively, was used by the parents of most of my friends.

Going out to play meant hours of freedom, particularly in the long summer holidays. Fairway and the roads round about had large numbers of young children; we were after all the baby boom generation so there was almost certainly someone to play with. If they were not on the streets then you only had to knock on a few doors asking, "Is Idris, (or Lesley, or Robert, or Kenny ...) coming out to play?"

On some occasions going out to play meant playing with one friend and on wet days it might mean playing indoors at their house or at home. More generally however large groups of us gathered on a corner and decided on a series of activities.

I am talking here about the period between the ages of around five and ten, the mid to late 1950s. There were, therefore, given our tender ages, certain key features of going out to play that would shock many modern parents and would be anathema to what is now generally a more risk averse culture with regard to child rearing practice.

The first was that there was no adult supervision. Children as young as five or six played outside with their friends. They organised the activities and they policed the rules of the games they played. Second, we were able to wander off to a local park or to meet friends who might live several streets away. Third, we received only minimal warnings about potential dangers, almost all relating to crossing the road carefully. The idea that paedophiles might be lurking behind every hedge was not a widely held belief in those days. And finally, we were often beyond the sight or control of our parents for large parts of the day.

So what did playing out look like? Of what did it consist?

There were gender based games, like skipping for girls and cricket or football for boys. However, the rules on this were pretty lax and girls might well join in cricket or football and we might well join in with their games. It has to be acknowledged however that while many girls could more than hold their own at the ball games, few boys, myself included, could cut the mustard at the skipping. The skipping was a mystery to most of us boys. We could just about manage individual skipping. What the girls could do was much more impressive. They used long ropes with complex patterns of joining in and disengaging. Each of these skipping games was accompanied by particular rhyming chants to which the girls kept rhythm. Two or more girls might be skipping on the long rope at one time and girls would swap from turning the rope to skipping with effortless ease. Occasionally, clearly awed but galled by the superior agility and coordination displayed, we boys would resort to spoiling tactics. Some things about the relationship between the genders do not change.

There were also mixed games like hide and seek, tig, London and "Farmer, farmer", dare, truth, kiss or promise, and postman's knock. London was an odd game as far as I can remember it. One person was nominated and she or he stood with their backs to the rest of us on the far side of the road. As this person chanted L-O-N-D-O-N we had to move forward across the road. On completing each chant he or she could turn quickly around. Anyone caught moving at this point would be sent back to the start. The aim was to move and freeze within the time of the chant and get across the road. It is a sport unlikely to be adopted as an Olympic event I fear.

"Farmer, farmer", was another chant game again setting the task of crossing the road. This time the person wanting to cross would chant, "Farmer, farmer may I cross your golden water?" The "farmer" would then say, "Not unless you show me something..." and would nominate a colour. The child would then have to show something in that colour that they were wearing or had about their person.

Tig was played in a variety of forms. The simplest was to nominate one person as "on". This person had to chase and touch or "tig" the others who dropped out of the round when caught. There were more sophisticated variations of this game, labelled "tig release". In one form a person who had been tigged had to freeze on the spot until released by being touched by another person. Even more demanding was a version where the release was effected only by going between the frozen person's legs.

Hide and seek always sounded like a better idea than it turned out. It carried a number of potential drawbacks. First, you ran the risk of hiding in the garden of one the few grumpy people who objected to having a child in their garden crouching behind the hedge. These people would knock on windows or come out to chase you away. They were invariably the same people who didn't give the ball back when the cricket shot or football kick sent it into their drive or garden. The second problem, and one it seems to me is intrinsic to the game, was that too much success was undesirable. You wanted to find a hiding place that would be seen as ingenious or obscure but if you did this too well you spent ages waiting and increasingly bored while they looked for you.

Dare, truth, kiss or promise and Postman's Knock were flirting games played by pre-pubescent children. They involved a great deal of squealing by girls and sounds of disgust by boys as they each pretended they had no desire to kiss the nominated member of the opposite sex or fulfil the often vaguely rude demand set as a dare or reveal the embarrassing facts demanded as a truth.

Football was a regular activity occasionally played in the local park but more often, particularly if time was tight, for example after school on a winter's afternoon, played on one of the larger semi-circular corner pavements in Fairway or Green Park Avenue. Sometimes twenty or more boys and girls would be crowded on this small space playing out a game usually with a tennis or similar sized ball. Passing was rare and the game usually comprised a mass scrimmage around the ball. The reluctance of most of us to go in goal was solved by the concept of the "rush back", literally the nominated player who would be expected to "rush back" from outfield play to save a shot. There were of course no referees. However, disputes were cut down by a large scale reduction in the number of offences that might be punished. There were no corners as space was too restricted. A throw in was given if the ball went into the road or someone's garden. Handball was about the only foul to be accepted without too much dispute and even then the perpetrator might claim they had taken over as "rush back goalie". Offside – well of course that was not applied even if we had known how to judge it. Played on a flagstone surface in short trousers, these games helped produce the scabby knees that seemed to be a permanent fixture to most boys' anatomies.

Cricket again might be played at a local park but more often was set up in the road. The corner was not big enough for a pitch, a problem solved by playing across the road with the bowler on one side and the batsman the other. The wicket would be chalked onto a wall or one of the wall support towers would be used. Everyone got a turn batting and bowling. LBW was abandoned and the only grounds for dismissal were bowled, caught or run-out. The umpiring decision was determined by the general response of players to any appeal made. A very democratic if not necessarily sound approach to decision making but certainly cheaper than Hawk Eye, Hot Spot or the Snickometer. Variants of the game were sometimes brought in to spice it up. 'Tip and run' meant that any contact with the ball by the batsman had to be followed by an attempted run. French cricket meant that the batter could be surrounded by bowlers all trying to hit his or her legs with the ball while he or she defended with the bat.

There were of course other games, marbles, played less often than might have been expected though the collection of marbles was an activity in itself. There was the seasonal game of conkers with its many secrets for success including pickling the conker. None of these recipes ever succeeded for me. One staple ingredient for playing out was a bike. These were almost always second-hand or hand-me-down machines. Most of us inherited bikes too big for us that we had to grow into. Cycling was rarely engaged in as an end in itself, it was rather a vehicle for the imagination. We played buses making the appropriate engine noises including the rapid change of tone as gears were shifted up in pulling away from a stop and, of course, the bell was employed for stopping and starting. We also used bikes as fighter planes, Spitfires of course, with a folded cigarette packet fixed into the spokes to make the sound of the machine guns.

Playing out was regulated by meal times and preparation for bed. Mothers would appear at the door of their houses to call in their children or would send a message via one of the other boys or girls. All being well the meal would be followed by a reappearance on the street. The final call was for bed. If we wandered too far or went near to the main road and were seen it would be reported to our parents and this would lead to a suspension of playing out rights. But on the whole we had a great deal of freedom. It is this freedom that many children have lost today. There are far more toys for them to play with and modern parents are often far more assiduous in providing a range of regular activities for their children. However, the key here perhaps is that the parents now provide these activities for their children and they plan, regulate and supervise them. Effectively the parents are in control. In trying to provide a richer range of things to entertain and stimulate their children there is the danger that children are being denied the opportunity to develop their own innate capacity to entertain and stimulate themselves. Children, in these programmes of activities, are also being kept in an environment designed by adults and controlled by them.

Of course any remembered experience, particularly one from a distant childhood and even more so one involving play, is subject to the distortion of sentimentality. I have little doubt that in my memory the episodes of playing out have been extended in time and enriched in the quality of experience by the warm glow of nostalgia. However, when I look back with as critical an eye as I can manage certain key features and merits still remain. We were given a level of control over our time and play that was enormously valuable. We had to mediate our relationships with a wide range of local children, some of whom were our friends and some of whom were not. We learned to compromise between what we wanted and what the consensus of opinion on that day decided. We invented or adapted the rules of games to suit the constraints of numbers, skills, equipment and environment. Most important of all, we were able, for a time at least, to inhabit a world comprising our peers free, or relatively free, from the control of adults. I for one am immensely grateful for that freedom.

8

Christmas

I AM STANDING at the top of a narrow, dark staircase staring down to the tiny hallway which is lit from the living room. It is my grandparents' house and I can be no more than four years old. I am struggling to carry what appears to be a huge sack filled with presents. That is all I recall of that early Christmas and yet, disconnected as it is from any wider context, it is a real memory, sharp and wonderfully evocative of all that Christmas came to represent or promise.

> You need to write your letter to Father Christmas. Don't forget to put "Dear Santa" at the start and "yours sincerely" at the end and don't forget to say "please" and "thank you". And remember, Father Christmas may not have all the toys you ask for. Then we will post it up the chimney.

Mum had an extraordinary gift for engaging the small child; for making the mundane exciting and interesting; the impossible credible. She also took these opportunities to reinforce useful conventions and good manners.

A Christmas tradition can be created in about three years. That at least is my theory when applied to young children. What I mean by this is that the way a family does something at Christmas becomes *the* Christmas tradition, the way things are done and the way they should be done for the child who experiences it. The child may reject this later of course, they may model their Christmases as an adult around other ideas they have come across, perhaps a partner's expectations for example. They may even model their adult Christmases as a direct rejection of what they experienced as children. However, whatever happens later, these early Christmases run deep in the memory and constitute for many of us the sense we have of Christmas past. My experience is no exception.

I have no idea whether or not the annual complaint that Christmas starts earlier every year has any basis in fact. Nor do I have any real grasp now of the kind of time-scale I am about to describe. The first inkling of Christmas took place for me as a child a long time before the actual event. I can see now my grandmother fastening strings to a series of muslin covered white bowls that were then lowered into the boiler in her kitchen. Prior to that event observed, I seem to remember, by as many members of the family as possible, was the mixing of the puddings. A rich, fruity aroma filled the kitchen. All of us got a turn at stirring the mixture with its heady fumes of alcohol. The mixture would then be spooned into the bowls, one for each of the families, and a sixpence dropped into each one. After boiling which I seem to remember, though this may be a fancy of the imagination, took place overnight, the bowls were drawn out and stored in my grandma's larder. I loved this event though ironically I never liked Christmas pudding. It was a tradition, and whether or not it went back two or three years or spanned generations I have no idea, but for me it was intrinsic to the whole concept of Christmas.

Then Christmas would be forgotten, revived only when someone said something like;

– It's incredible to think that there are only thirty more shopping days to Christmas.

For me the next key event and the true marker of the Christmas season beginning was the arrival of Father Christmas at Lewis's in Bull Street. There were of course other pretenders to the real throne of Father Christmas, including a convincing claimant at the Co-op in Northfield, but the Lewis's incarnation was the real thing according to my mum. Santa's grotto, filled with elves, and other furnishings from Lapland, appeared huge to me. At the end of the trip along the grotto you got to sit on Santa's knee. He usually asked what you wanted for Christmas and for an assurance that you would be a good boy. He then dipped into his sack and brought out a present. Father Christmas at Lewis's had an assistant, or I confusedly thought at the time, a brother, called Uncle Holly. While Father Christmas wore a red outfit Uncle Holly wore a green suit and top hat like some kind of grotesquely oversized leprechaun.

Father Christmas had a pretty demanding job. Not only did he have to appear in person at Lewis's for several weeks right up to and including Christmas Eve, he also had to quality assure his deputies who appeared in his place at other shops. From mum's explanation, in answer to my questions about these other Father Christmases in other stores, emerged a version of the franchise model. But this of course was only the prelude to his real work. Probably in the evenings or on Sundays, mum would explain, he had to supervise the packing and loading of presents ready for delivery on Christmas Eve. Then he had to visit all the homes in the world with children over a period of a few hours, leaving a sack of presents at the end of each bed. All this with a vehicle drawn by flying reindeer. Calculations have been done since of the required speed for such an epic venture and they seem to involve a velocity approaching or exceeding the speed of light. Such mundane scientific considerations did not enter my mind at the time.

What did however confuse me was the fact that there appeared to be two different versions of the origin of presents. A parallel, perhaps, to the fact that many scholars believe that two different traditions of the Creation have been conflated in Genesis. The first, and earlier origin of the presents story, posited that all presents come from Father Christmas. In choosing these presents he takes account, but cannot be expected to adhere rigidly to, the letter of request sent to him up the chimney a few weeks earlier. This is a straight forward account and made eminent sense to me. At some stage however, probably with the onset of literacy, a problem arose. Each present had attached to it a label. On the label, in patently different handwriting for each one, it would say;

"To Peter
Love from
Auntie Joan, Grandma and Granddad, Uncle Geoff and Auntie Peggy..." and so on.

How could this be explained? Mum, who missed her vocation as either a post-modernist novelist or a Scriptural critic, came up with a number of possible answers. The multiplicity of her answers may have reflected the complexity of the issue, the limitation of human knowledge, the fertility of her imagination or the fact that she forgot she had given me a different answer to the same question at an earlier date.

Version one: all presents were from Father Christmas but were assigned on request as being from specific relatives.

Version two: the presents were bought by the relatives and then sent to Father Christmas for delivery.

Version three: the sack contained a mixture of presents directly from Father Christmas, assigned presents delivered by Father Christmas and a few delivered directly from the relatives to my parents for inclusion in the sack.

There was then the problem of access. The traditional story says that Father Christmas comes down the chimney to deliver presents.

– Mum, Paul Hodgkiss in my class lives in a flat and they have no chimney. How will he get his presents?

– Father Christmas has a special key that will get him into any house in the world.

Thank goodness for his honesty given such a device!
Exactly one week before Christmas Day, a tree would be bought. Our trees always had roots and one of mum's doctrinal rules was that

artificial trees were unacceptable under pretty well all circumstances. The decorations for the tree and rooms were brought down from the attic. All of us then helped out in the ritual of decoration.

On Christmas Eve my parents always had a lot to organise and we were sent off to bed early with the stern injunction that Father Christmas would not visit until we were asleep. Yet another complication and potential delay to his already demanding delivery programme! Despite the firm command to sleep it did not come. One year Richard, aged about three, shouted out the question every few minutes from his cot;

– Is it Christmas yet?

At some point I fell asleep and awoke in the dark of the early morning. I crawled to the end of the bed and began to fumble in the dark in the sack trying to guess from the shape of the packages. Eventually at some unearthly hour my parents admitted defeat and allowed us to begin opening presents. The practice in our family, one I came to firmly reject as an adult and parent, was to open the presents in our own rooms, accompanied by a running, shouted commentary on what we had and who had sent it. Sometimes in the excitement, labels would not be read before a present was opened and no record would remain of who had sent what. This would then be followed by detective work by mum.

A letter had to be sent to all present givers. Wherever possible it was required that a specific reference be made to the present chosen and an acknowledgement offered as to why this item was particularly welcomed;

Dear Auntie and Uncle
Thank you so much for the lovely socks. They are exactly what I wanted as most of my socks have holes in them. I hope you had a lovely Christmas.
Love
Peter

In the event of no sender being identified the letter would be more generic in tone;

Dear Auntie and Uncle
Thank you so much for your lovely present. It is exactly what I wanted. I had a lovely Christmas and I hope you did too.
Love
Peter

Presents had a strict hierarchy in my mind. At the apex were toys. Followed closely by games and books. A long way behind these came clothes. Bottom came money. Not because I did not want money but because it was my mum's strict view that offering money showed "a lack of thought".

What presents stand out in memory? There was a castle handmade by my Uncle Tony in recognition of my interest in history and to provide a base for my collection of plastic knights. It was made of plywood but had been painted grey and coated with a textured surface to simulate rough stone. There were towers at each corner and aside the gate and a drawbridge which was lowered by tiny chains. It was magnificent. There was a huge wooden game from Uncle Geoff and Auntie Peggy. In it metal balls were propelled by a spring loaded mechanism and were caught in small traps, each with a different value. Dad and his brothers spent more time playing with it than me that Christmas.

Then there was the bike. This was the most exciting present I ever had. I had longed for a bike but had been told that the cost was too high. I arose that Christmas morning and came down stairs. There in the front room next to the Christmas tree was a shiny blue bike on its stand. I climbed on and pedalled furiously as it rocked precariously from side to side. I had not yet learned to ride but my father held onto the saddle as I rode all the way to my grandparents that afternoon, a journey of about three miles, it must have been backbreaking for him especially as there was the return trip late that night. After days of practice and several falls I was able to greet dad on his return from work one evening riding unsupported if rather erratically. Years later I learned that my parents, unable to afford the cost of a new bike, had acquired a second-hand one. Through a relative who worked in a factory it had been resprayed and new fittings had been attached. Dad had worked through to the small hours of Christmas morning assembling the parts. Looking back I can only hope that my obvious delight was repayment for this effort.

Finally, there was the crystal set. This was less obviously exciting than the bike but in its impact no less dramatic. It was a kit. My dad and I put it together and then, with the long wire aerial out of the window, we tried it out. As we tuned it in I could hear through the headphones the hum and whistle of distant stations until at last it picked up the Home Service. That afternoon I listened enthralled to a dramatisation of *The Hound of the Baskervilles,* my first introduction to Conan Doyle, the beginning of a lifelong pleasure. Soon a habit of listening late into the night, often beneath the blankets, was established and I was to gain access to such gems as Al Reid, *Hancock's Half Hour* and numerous dramas and serialised books.

Mum worked hard throughout the morning preparing the Christmas dinner. We always had the meal as a nuclear family. The centre piece of the meal was a roast and stuffed chicken. This was accompanied by sprouts, boiled to a pulp in the best tradition of those times, internal and external stuffing and other varied vegetables with, of course, roast potatoes. I do not recall either cranberry or bread sauce. This meal, uniquely in the year, was served with wine for the adults though we were allowed a taste. In early years the wine of choice was Spanish Sauterne. This wine was not to be confused with the genuine French variety that can easily fetch hundreds of pounds a bottle. The clue perhaps is in the additional adjective, "Spanish". This variety was a white wine with lots of added sugar. Clearly meant to be drunk as a dessert wine it was favoured by my parents for the main course. Later, probably under the influence of Berni Inns, this was replaced by Blue Nun and later still by Mateus Rose.

Christmas pudding was then brought in, flaming with that distinctive blue flame of ignited brandy. It was served with Birds Custard. Mince pies were offered as a sop to those of us who did not like Christmas pud.

After dinner had been cleared we dressed up and set off, wearing as many items of clothing that had been sent as presents as would fit together. Richard and I were allowed to take a select sample of presents with us. We then walked across to Cliff Rock Road, Rednal, where the wider family gathered for tea and where other members of the more extended family dropped in at some time during the evening. It was usual for the four daughters, their husbands and children to be present along with granddad's spinster sisters, Ada and Edie. There were then visits from my grandparents' siblings, nephews and nieces. The men drank whisky in most cases and the women sherry, port or Babychamp, the latter a revoltingly sickly sweet imitation of champagne that was seen as the height of sophistication along with Advocaat. Late in the evening we set out, tired but happy, for home.

Boxing Day was our turn to be the hosts. My maternal grandparents came across for dinner, a meal always served at what might now be called lunchtime. Then for the rest of the afternoon and evening relatives from both sides of the family called in for drinks and snacks. Those with cars were invariably offered, "One for the road."

Dad was back at work on the day after Boxing Day and this was the time when the new toys were played with. It was also the time to read books that had been bought and in particular to look through the annuals. Each year for several years I received the *Rupert Bear Annual* with its wonderfully evocative pictures of an idyllic English landscape within which the most exotic of adventures would be played out by Rupert and his pals. I also received the annuals of the three comics I read each week, *The Topper*, *The Beano* and *The Dandy*.

Then it was all over. The tree, dropping ever more needles onto the floor, was finally taken out and planted in the garden in the ever vain hope that it would take root and be available for next year. All over and leaving me always with that slight sense of melancholy that the ending of things so often produces for me: the end of festivals, holidays, school years, jobs. Each ending is a micro-cosmic reminder perhaps that nothing lasts. At least that is the grand version of the interpretation. Perhaps it was simply the natural sense of lowering after the unsustainable high of Christmas.

9

The Tiger in the Smoke

AN ALMOST annual feature of autumn and winter in the 1950s was smog. Smog was the result of the combination of cold temperatures, low wind speed, heavy fog and the huge quantity of smoke and soot produced by domestic fires and factories. Almost all houses were heated by coal fires. In the winter there were hundreds of thousands of such fires in Birmingham and the West Midlands pouring sulphurous smoke out into the atmosphere. On most days the effect of this was visible and the smoke would climb up into the sky or be blown away by the wind. However, when a lethal combination of conditions occurred the smoke would be held in the air. The impact was devastating.

There is a whole genre of literature and historical accounts that depend on the smog for atmosphere. The sense of the unseen threat that might lurk in the dense smog enhances the horror of Jack the Ripper, Spring Heeled Jack or the Sherlock Holmes stories. One of the finest examples is Margaret Allingham's *The Tiger in the Smoke*. Its greatest poetic realisation is in T.S. Eliot's, *The Love Song of J Alfred Prufrock*;

"The yellow fog that rubs its back against the window-panes
The yellow smoke that rubs it muzzle on the window-panes..."

It provides the setting for the magnificent opening of Dickens's *Bleak House*. Smog made for atmosphere in books, poems or films and is even romanticised in song as in Gershwin's;

"A foggy day in London town......"

But in reality it was appalling and there was little that was romantic or excitingly atmospheric about it.

The most famous of the smogs was in 1952 in London and it lasted for five days. It virtually paralysed the life and economy of the city. It was said to have been responsible for the deaths of over 4000 people and such was its impact that it led to a debate that finally resulted in the Clean Air Act of 1956.

It is difficult now to imagine what it was like to experience a smog unless you visit somewhere like Beijing. Which is not to say of course that our cities are not still plagued by pollution. They are but the modern pollutants are largely invisible. Smog was very visible. It appeared as a dense wall a few feet or even inches in front of your face. You were enveloped by a yellowy brown miasma that swirled around you as you moved through it. The shapes of buildings, cars, buses, lamp-posts and people loomed out of the dense smog, their outlines blurred, their colours entirely obscured. Artificial light had almost no ability to penetrate it. The headlamps of buses or cars seemed to be reflected back or diffused. It had a powerfully disorientating effect. The familiar became unfamiliar, alien. You were no longer able to recognise known local landmarks. Locating where you were and which direction you were heading became almost impossible. Parents were advised to keep children indoors because of the risk of getting lost or having an accident. The internal lights of houses or buses would appear momentarily, suspended in the air, apparently disconnected from any solid body. The yellow light they cast was sickly and weak with no power to lighten the space around it.

Then there was the smell. The smog carried the intense odour of ice cold sulphur. In a long lasting smog that might linger for days it got into everything. Your clothes and hair stank of smoke. It got in through the doors and your home began to smell of the smog. It left a thin yellow film like some noxious snail slime.

It muffled sound, and combined with the fact that you could not see more than a few feet, it dislocated your capacity to place the origin of the noises you could hear. Everything appeared and sounded immediate. The usual sense of perspective was lost. A shape, a light, a sound, appeared suddenly and immediately before you and then disappeared with the same ghostly effect. Smog created a surreal world in which bus conductors walked slowly before buses holding flaming torches, their features briefly lit as they moved past you before the light faded into a dull and diffused glow suspended in the air, disconnected from any person or object. As you walked you stumbled down or up kerbs. You were uncertain whether you were on the pavement or the road. Journeys that normally took minutes took hours. Buses sometimes gave up on the struggle and everyone had to get off and walk.

There were times when my father walked from the city centre to our home, a distance of over seven miles, in order to get back from work. People you passed, who appeared suddenly before you, leaned forward to peer into the obscurity, hands clasping scarves to their mouths and noses.

Inside you felt cocooned by the smog. There was no distinction between night and day. Lights were on permanently. The house lights could not illuminate the outside, you could see only your reflection in the window. It was as if the world beyond the window had ceased to exist. As if you were floating in the smog itself.

Football fixtures were postponed. Schools were closed, something that rarely happened for even the most extreme snow falls. Deliveries of milk and bread were severely disrupted. The smog was the dominant feature of life for the days it lasted.

As a child I thought the natural colour of most public and large buildings, particularly those clad in marble or stone, was a grimy black. Visit the lovely Georgian City of Bath today and you will see buildings of a rich honey or grey stone. When I passed through it on our regular trips to East Woodlands in the 50s or 60s, the noble buildings were black. Visiting London for my eighth or ninth birthday, the dome of St Paul's and the White Tower appeared to me as grim, blackened structures.

Smog in the 1950s seemed a fact of life. Each year it would appear. Sometimes for a few hours, sometimes a whole day and night and occasionally for days on end. While it was there it was the single overwhelming feature of life. It affected all our senses, dislocated all normal life, and distorted our very perception of the world around us. Then it was gone and we awaited its next appearance. The Clean Air Act of 1956, legislated for a gradual phasing out of coal as a domestic source of heat. It took time and smogs lingered into the early sixties. There was a shift first to cleaner, so called smokeless fuels, then as the years went on gas, electric or oil fired central heating replaced coal fires and the smogs became a thing of the past.

10

And so to school:
Part 2 – Secondary School

Dear Sir or Madam
I am now able to tell you that in the light of the performance of
your child in the Birmingham Junior School Leaving Exam-
ination it will be possible (subject to verification of date of birth)
to offer him a place in Bilateral, Comprehensive, Commercial,
Grammar or Technical School in September next....
   Yours faithfully,
   E. Russell
   Chief Education Officer

HAVING passed my 11-plus I gained a place at King
Edward's Five Ways. I had not visited the school before
applying so I really had no idea what to expect. In
September 1961 when I started Five Ways the Bartley Green site was
only three years old and had the feel still of a very new building. The
school sports' field was not yet ready for use and so a weekly trip
had to be made to George Dixon School on the City Road,
Edgbaston, for games periods.

The school was approached for most pupils from the direction of
Northfield or Quinton or the city centre on buses that ran through
the suburban sprawl of south west Birmingham. However, across

Scotland Lane which fronted the school was waste land that backed onto woods and fields and beyond that Frankley Church and Frankley Beeches and miles of countryside. To the right of the school as viewed from Scotland Lane was the reservoir with its long low dam and small, gothic styled pumping houses. From many school classrooms the view was distinctly rural and the setting provided us with the most genuinely rural cross-country course of any school in the city at that time.

The first visit to the school was an evening introduction. An address to parents by the head teacher, Mr Burgess, of which I remember precisely nothing. This was followed by fittings for school uniform and sports kit. The head of PE, Mr Carter, took one look at me and stated that there was not much to me and recommended the smallest sizes for PE vest, shorts and rugby shirts. We had two rugby shirts, one plain white and one hooped black and white, thus allowing us to engage in competitive team games in school.

This first visit was followed by the first day. I was given a lift to school by dad. The school uniform: black shoes, grey socks with black and white hoops at the top, grey shorts, grey or white shirt, black and white striped tie, black blazer with the school badge and a hooped black and white cap, conspired to make me look even more puny than I was. This was not helped by mum's policy of buying clothes "to grow into". Generally this meant months, if not years, of wearing clothes that appeared to be borrowed from a much older child and which hung off me. The school policy stated that it was expected that boys would wear short trousers up to and including the third year (Year 9 in new money). This ruling was more honoured in the breech than the observance and many boys were in long trousers from the start, many more by Year 2 and all but three or four by the start of Year 3. I was of course one of the three or four as mum's view was that if that was what the policy said that is what it meant and besides which there was still plenty of wear in the shorts yet.

We were assigned to three forms, 1A for those who had obviously come with the best pass marks, 1E for the those who were born in the first half of the school year and 1Y for those born in the second half of the year. I was in 1Y. We were also allocated to the four Houses, Bates, McPhersons, Rants and Roses. My parents had asked if I could be allocated to McPhersons as that was the House my Uncle Tony had been in when he was at the school in the 1930s. We were seated alphabetically with Abbot and Abrams front row by the door and on round to the far left row where I was seated with Stevenson, Thomas, Tomkins and others with names at the latter end of the alphabet.

Day one was just for the first years. It comprised: an introduction to our form tutor, Mr Scott, who would also be our history teacher; guided tours of the buildings; the handing out of books; and the repeated reinforcement of school rules. All very gentle and secure.

Day two came therefore as a shock. In my pristine if gargantuan uniform including its firmly affixed cap, I entered the school grounds to be greeted by giants who clearly regarded all first years, or "fags" as they called us, particularly small ones, as fair game. Caps were not for wearing but for the entertainment of older boys who would snatch them, pass them around or throw them across the playground. Prodding, tripping, and threatening were all regarded as good clean fun and the more fear shown the better and the greater the invitation to escalate the fun. If the playground was a place that inspired trepidation, the toilets inspired terror. The smell of cigarette smoke was all pervasive and the intimidation reached far higher levels here. Bullying, for that is what it was beneath all the veneer of a time-honoured tradition, was largely tolerated by teachers as long as no major physical damage was done, and was accepted by us as part of the initiation ceremony. We would have our year as victims then it would be our turn to become the source of fear.

The school was clearly influenced in many ways, as were so many grammar schools in those days, by the traditions of Public Schools. There was a Founder's Prayer that was recited every Friday:

We give Thee most humble and hearty thanks, O most merciful Father, for our pious founder King Edward VI and

all our governors and benefactors by whose benefit this whole
school is brought up to Godliness and good-learning, and we
humbly beseech Thee to give us grace to use these Thy
blessings to the glory of Thy holy name that we may answer
the good intent of our religious founder and become
profitable members of the Church and Commonwealth and
at last be partakers of Thy heavenly kingdom. Through our
Lord and Saviour Jesus Christ.

Amen

Assembly each morning began with the Head Boy going up a few
steps by the raised stage at the front of the hall and by a hand gesture
bidding the whole school to rise to its feet as the head master entered
the hall. Along each side of the hall were the prefects and sub-
prefects, the prefects wearing their white braided blazers. Assembly
comprised hymns, prayers, a Bible reading either by a member of
staff or a prefect, any presentations that might be made that day,
some words from the head and then the Head Boy gestured us to
stand and the head would depart.

At this point, we resumed out seats and the deputy head would
then deliver some harangue about poor behaviour; generally known
by us as "a good bollocking". The deputy who succeeded Sam Hin-
ton, Mr Eyles, had a speech defect and could not pronounce his "r"s
or "l"s. This led to him being irreverently nicknamed "Toffee Eyles".
This was particularly pronounced in one of the prayers that he would
often recite in assemblies when he deputised for the head master;

– "To wabour without weward…"

On one notable occasion he stepped forward and launched into
us;

– It has come to my notice that some bwoys when pwaying
football are climbing onto the woof to retwieve their bawlls. This is
a dangerous pwactice and one that endangers not only their pwerson
but also scwool pwoperty. It is to cease fwom this time. I hope I
make myself cwear.

A large fifth former standing at the back (fifth and sixth formers stood in assembly) who happened to have a perforated ear-drum and so could not judge the volume of his speech, suddenly said in what he imagined to be a witty and quiet aside to his neighbours;

– In other words, weave your balls on the woof.

There was a stunned silence. Such was Mr Eyles' reputation that no one laughed, no one giggled. Mick Jones, the offending lad, was clearly horrified and spluttered some lines to his neighbours. An outraged Mr Eyles, roared;

– Who said that? Who is that bwoy?

Jones was quickly identified as the culprit and ordered to Mr Eyles' room where no doubt he received a good caning.

At primary school I had gone home for lunch each day as mum worked in the evenings and was thus available for the mid-day meal. This was not possible at secondary school as the distance was too great so I stayed for school lunch. Tickets were sold each day in the form period. At lunchtime a queue was formed alongside the hall. In the dining area behind the hall we sat on tables of twelve. Tickets were collected by the head of table and lads near the top of the table collected the meals in metals tins from the kitchen hatch. They then served the meals to the rest of the table. This was an opportunity for minor levels of corruption. The top of table boys were generally older and bigger and felt it was a legitimate perk of the job to take the lion's share of the meal for themselves. In later years I was one of those who headed a table and I am afraid that I cannot say I set an example of fair and just behaviour in this respect.

The meals varied in quality. Chips and shepherd's pie were regarded as first rate as were the roast potatoes and meat pies. For dessert, treacle or jam steam puddings, crumble and pies were highly valued as was rice pudding. Salads and tapioca were generally despised. Occasionally the mash had hard blue bits in it.

One meal time in my first year the physics teacher Mr Williams was on duty. He was known occasionally to stand over fussy eaters and make sure they downed every morsel. Polished table manners were not a distinguishing feature of meal times. One day Mr Williams, appalled by a display of particularly crass behaviour shouted at one table that;

– My dog has better manners than you lot!

To which a quick witted lad responded;

– Yes sir, but your dog probably gets better food.

To give him credit Mr Williams joined in the laughter rather than punishing the boy.

Occasionally in carrying a pile of plates to or from a table an accident would happen and plates would fall and smash with a resounding crash. This would be met by the inevitable cheers from the boys and shouts of "Silence!" from the staff on duty.

Staff took their lunches not in the dining room but in the hall. They were served by a group of boys from the fourth year who volunteered to do this job for the year. I was such a volunteer. Why would anyone volunteer for such a job? Very simple – because you got more food and more time to eat it in some peace when the masters had finished. Furthermore, we regarded it as perfectly acceptable to tax the masters by skimming off delicacies such as roast potatoes and chips which were then stored away for our meals. On the way to and from the kitchens with the food trolly we sup- plemented our meals by picking at the choice dishes.

Corporal punishment was an integral part of the school discipline code. Generally there were three levels. The lowest was the administration of casual cuffs to the head or the tugging of ears by masters as they patrolled the lesson. The second level was slippering. Masters kept a gym pump in their desk drawer and offenders were called out front, made to bend over and slippered as many times as the master felt appropriate. The highest and most formal level was caning. This was administered, as far as I remember, only by the head master or deputy head master.

Although all masters could and usually did hand out slipperings, the deterrent effect depended heavily on the reputation of the master as a slipperer. In my day, Mr Butler and Mr Lloyd were much feared in this respect; Mr Lloyd for his technique and Mr Butler for his brute strength.

I was not a particularly difficult boy but I was slippered on many occasions and I had the dubious honour of being the first in my class to receive this punishment. It was in geography in the first few weeks and was at the hands of Mr Mandry. Tired of the fact that every time he asked a question the enthusiastic boys in class not only put up their hands but cried out, "Sir, sir!" to attract his attention. After warning us about this he issued his ultimatum;

– The next boy who yells out instead of quietly putting his hand up, gets the slipper.

Next question and I knew the answer. Before I could stop myself out it came;

– Sir, s...!

– Right Traves, out here and bend over.

In later years one of the commonest reasons for me being slippered was the fact that my best friend Mark Stevenson looked old enough, or at least convinced the cinema staff at the Warley Odeon to believe he was old enough, to watch X rated horror films. How did this lead to my being slippered? Well, in double science with Mr Johnson I would beg Mark to tell me the story of the latest horror film he had seen.

– So there's this grave and they're opening it up...

– Traves and Stevenson, be quiet and get on with your work!

– Sorry sir.

– Go on Mark he's not looking. Then what happened?

– The coffin opens and...

– It's the last time I'm telling you two.

– Sorry sir.

– Mark, Mark! Then what?

– It's really dark. The lid opens and out comes...

– Right that's it! Traves and Stevenson out here.

Five Ways was at that time an all boys school. This meant that talk of girls took place almost exclusively in terms of sex, a subject on which for most of our schooling most of us had little or no direct experience. There was a local girls' grammar school, Bartley Green, and this became for many us in the years before we started to go out to clubs and dances the focal point of our fantasies. One day in the fourth year in the first lesson of the afternoon, I overheard excited talk amongst a pair of my friends, Colin Morris and Mitch Price, hinting at something remarkable that had happened over the lunch break.

    – It was incredible though wasn't it Col?

    – Yeah. I can't believe it really. I never thought they'd go that far. Did you?

    – I can't wait till tomorrow.

Mark, sitting next to me, turned sharply to them;

    – We promised not to say anything. So you need to shut up about it.

    – What...not even to Pete?

    – Not even to Pete.

Nothing is more likely to arouse curiosity than the hint of a secret to be revealed and then withheld. For the rest of the afternoon I begged them to let me in on this. Colin was of the view that an exception should be made in my case. Mark argued that a promise had been given and that not even a good friend like Pete should be let in on this. I pleaded. I made more and more solemn promises of secrecy if told. I made my case on the basis of their friendship and of being offended that they would not trust me. Eventually, Mitch and Colin agreed I should be told and Mark despite his profound reservations gave way.

During lunch they said they had been over on the far side of the playing fields by the fence that bordered on to Genners Lane behind the school. A group of girls from Bartley Green School had been going past and had responded to their calls. They had got into conversation with these girls who had then joined them on the slopes of the field out of sight of the school. One thing had led to another and eventually various sexual favours had been offered and gratefully accepted. At every stage of the account I was reminded of my solemn promise to keep all this a secret. The girls had arranged to come the next day at about the same time. I was agog with interest and excitement. Could I join them the next day? At first again there was stern refusal. But eventually they said I could.

I hardly slept that night with excitement and showed an unusual keenness for school the next morning. The lessons before lunch seemed to crawl by but at last the bell went, a rapid meal was consumed and I joined my three friends on the far side of the field. Groups of girls appeared, passed and went on their way.

– Is this them? Is this them?

– Could be...not sure...no.

Another group.

– Is this them?

– Yes, I think it is...no.

The minutes passed still no sign and my hopes of a somewhat limited and probably very squalid orgy began to fade. Then I was aware of the sound of helpless laughter from my friends. I looked at them at first bewildered until it became increasingly clear. The whole thing from start to finish, from the first hints to the eventual narrative of sexual activity, had been a scam, a practical joke at my expense.

– You bastards!

But swallowing my sense of gullibility and my sexual dis-appointment, I had to admit it had been brilliantly performed.

Like most schools Five Ways had its mixture of teachers. There were many good teachers, a few who were sound but dull and a few who were unable to control classes. Clever boys were often ingenious, not to say merciless, at playing up. There were the standard activities, humming that would build up to a crescendo, lifting the desks on the knees so that they creaked and sometimes moving the whole row of desks forward each time the teacher turned to the board to that by the end of the lesson he was virtually pinned against the board. A few boys possessed a genuine talent for disruption that could reduce a teacher to frustrated impotence and a class to helpless laughter.

The passing of forty years seemed an impossible idea to me then but now its final verse, grossly sentimental though it might be and clearly reflecting the values of its nineteenth century Public School origin, has a poignancy that informs my memories of school and of my sense of a life largely lived as I approach old age. I am well past the forty years on point, in fact it is over fifty years since I started at Five Ways.

> "Forty years on, growing older and older,
> Shorter in wind, as in memory long,
> Feeble of foot, and rheumatic of shoulder,
> What will it help you that once you were strong?
> God give us bases to guard or beleaguer,
> Games to play out, whether earnest or fun;
> Fights for the fearless, and goals for the eager,
> Twenty, and thirty, and forty years on!"

11

This Sporting Life

SPORT WAS highly valued at Five Ways. Each week we had a timetabled gym lesson and a whole afternoon of games. We had excellent facilities. There were extensive playing fields with well-kept rugby pitches in winter and carefully tended cricket pitches and a grass athletics track in the summer. The gym was brand new and well equipped. There was an outdoor swimming pool of very modest size and three Eton Fives courts, of which more later.

There was however a pecking order of sports and, again I suspect influenced by the Public School tradition, rugby ruled supreme and in fact no football was played in school at all. At least not played officially. It was very different in the playground where a whole series of football games would be on the go every break and lunch time. The school's view was that rugby was for young gentlemen and football for the plebs. The fact that whenever we had the choice we played football may well say something about the social origins of most of the pupils, who were largely from plebeian rather than genteel backgrounds.

The playground was unofficially but very strictly divided into the pitches of different year groups. How this happened I have no idea but no one ever attempted to muscle in on the pitches of a different group. To an outsider observing from a vantage point above the playground it would have appeared entirely chaotic. Matches were played across each other. Large older boys running at speed made no concession for small younger boys in their way. Collisions were commonplace. But somehow or other it worked, or at least worked most of the time. The group I played with took as its pitch an area from the gym wall up towards the mini-tennis courts set out on the playground. Each break and lunchtime we selected teams and played. There were a few boys who even kept an account of how many goals they scored each term; even then we regarded that as a rather "sad" thing to do. We used the same space in summer for cricket and again the games of different groups overlapped.

I later learned to like rugby. Largely I have to say due to the years I spent in Wales where the sport was popular in its base and had none of the snobbery then associated with English rugby. At school however, with a few exceptions, I did not enjoy the rugby games I played. I was small in height and even smaller in build when I went to Five Ways. I had reasonable speed, good stamina and sound ball-handling skills but very limited aggression and fragile physical courage. I played hooker. It means being in the heart of the scrum in the middle of the front row. When the scrum goes down and the ball is put in by the scrum-half it is the hooker's job to hook the ball back with his, or perhaps nowadays, her foot so that it goes through the scrum on our side and we gain possession. Fine. Except it meant in my case being the smallest member of the pack by far but being at the fulcrum of pressure from the biggest and heaviest players in the side. I was fine at pack play in terms of actually hooking, in fact I was quite good at this aspect and was considered for the school team on this basis. My problem was loose play. I was fine at catching and passing. What I hated was tackling. Tackling invariably involved getting in the way of a big boy who was running fast and who had his brawny arm out to knock puny weaklings like me out of the way. I also regarded the frequent cry to "Fall on the ball" as being roughly similar to the cry "Fall on the sword" as it meant going down in the mud beneath the kicks and bodies of strong aggressive opponents and team-mates.

I made the school cricket team and captained the house team. There were those glorious summer days when whole afternoons would be spent out on the field playing cricket. There were also the typical English summer days when the ball flying to slips stung the freezing hands and when as much time was spent in the changing rooms hoping against hope that the clouds would clear and the rain stop.

Gym involved the use of all the equipment. Ropes, boxes, mats and wall bars and the systematic and skilful teaching of various techniques by Mr Carter and Mr Warner. There were the much enjoyed end of term games in the gym of crab football and pirates. The latter involved avoiding being caught by the designated catchers by moving rapidly around the gym across wall bars, ropes, mats and equipment avoiding at all cost touching the gym floor. Punishment in gym was enriched by the sentence to hang on the wall bars. This meant hanging by your hands from the top wall bar with feet held clear of the bars below. This sounds simple but after a very short time it was extremely painful. I have little doubt that this punishment would contravene the Human Rights Act! We however, accepted it as yet another quirk of the good old school. Changing times could be tricky as more belligerent boys thought it a great joke to flick wet towels at your naked back-side and the showers, compulsory as well as necessary, sometimes ran cold before you had finished with them.

The Fives Courts were a feature of the King Edward's schools in Birmingham. There are apparently two versions of the game played on very different courts – Eton and Rugby Fives, taking their names of course from the famous schools. We had Eton Fives. The courts are small with walls on three sides and open at the back. About a third of the way back from the front wall was a low step and a low angle topped wall ran along part of this step from the left. I imagine this replicates the original Eton building where the game was played. The game has features in common with squash except that it is played with a gloved hand and the ball is hard. It is, despite its esoteric nature a fast, skilful and highly enjoyable game to play and I turned out to have a modicum of talent for it. Courts could be booked for the lunch break and after school. House competitions were held and there was a school team that had a handful of fixtures each year against the few schools that played the game in the Midlands.

I had always been a runner. Sent down the road to post a letter or to buy a few provisions, I would treat the journey as a race on which I commentated in my head. In these fictional races I was unbeaten and had accrued several Olympic gold medals and a number of world records by the end of my primary school years. I had however, never taken part in a real and organised cross-country race. One Wednesday morning in gym during my first term it was decided that the form would have its first cross-country race. We were shown the route and we lined up in the playground and set off. Out across the front playing field, over Scotland Lane and onto a track leading into the woods. Through the woods and out again onto the road alongside the reservoir.

Up to this point I had been jogging along chatting to a group of friends, however, for some reason I decided at this moment to make an effort. I accelerated up the road, right at the T-junction and on past Frankley Church and then over a stile across a ploughed field. Another stile and a steep climb up a grassy hill to a third stile. By this time I was in third position. Around the edge of a ploughed field then as we went down hill towards Scotland Lane I moved up into second position. On into the school grounds to finish across the playground. I had completed the course in a respectable 15 minutes and 17 seconds and was second behind David (Tich) Loynes. Considering that I had made only a nominal effort for the first third of the run it was a good achievement. My father asked that evening how I had done and then announced that he was not surprised as he knew I would do well. His response delighted me and added to my pleasure. From then on cross-country became my main winter sport. I ran for the school for almost seven years and after school I continued to run for clubs and later simply for pleasure and fitness.

Birmingham had a vibrant cross-country league for schools in those days. There were some top class young runners in the city

*Five Ways junior and intermediate cross-country teams 1962-63.
Left to right with Mr Hughes (back left) and Mr Butler (back right)
Front row: Newbold, Traves, Harrison, Latimer, Worrall.*

including the Stewart brothers who would go on to win international track fame. There were some demanding courses and in winter, running as we did in shorts and gym vests, it could be a pretty arduous affair as we ploughed through mud and crossed the occasional icy stream. I particularly remember the winter of 1962-63 when snow lay on the ground for sixty-two consecutive days, by far the longest on record. Schools rarely if ever closed for bad weather in those days and, though a few fixtures were postponed, the cross-country season continued. In one race at Colmore Farm School the course took us through a stream. The weather was ferociously cold that day and I can vividly remember lads reduced to tears of pain in the changing rooms as their frozen feet warmed and circulation was restored.

Five Ways in my view had the toughest, most varied and most attractive courses. At senior level the course took you up a track and then across fields to the top of Frankley Beeches. Then after this climb you came back down onto the road and looped back to

Frankley Church to climb again. Psychologically it was hard for visiting teams as they began to realise that they were heading back for a second dose of what must have been one of the hardest climbs on any Midland's course.

The pecking order of sports was rubbed in when we were invited to host a major schools' championship. This was a source of pride for the team but it came to nothing because the rugby second XV had a home game that week and this was judged to take precedence over cross-country. Strange how these things stay in the memory; this sense of an injustice which though small ranged large for young boys who turned out week after week to represent the school in this unglamorous sport and who developed a strong sense of team spirit.

The cross-country teams for most of my time in the school were run by Mr Hughes, a young Welsh science teacher. He was an enthusiastic advocate for the sport and a kind and decent man. The team respected him and wanted to do its best for him. We did however attempt to mimic in his South Wales accent his favourite refrain;

– Remember lads – get a good start!

I enjoyed racing, particularly in those races where I performed well, but what I remember with most pleasure were those runs, perhaps in games lessons or perhaps for practice, when I was out there running within myself, a seemingly effortless running that can only be described as a source of delight to those who are or have been runners. Because of a chronic illness I can no longer run but sometimes at night I dream that I am running with the old ease. Sadly when I awake I realise all too quickly that it is just a dream.

12

Extended Families

Members of both extended families at Cliff Rock Road early 1950s.

I T WAS always "our Pete". It was as if the plural possessive pronoun was part of my name. In part of course it's a feature of West Midland's speech: "our mum", "our house" "our kid". It felt more than this however. It felt like a statement of belonging to the wider extended family.

Dad's family brought together the Traves and the Coltmans. My paternal grandfather's family had their origins in the South West but had been in Wolverhampton certainly since the mid-nineteenth century. My grandmother's family was from County Durham, a mining family from the Chester-le-Street area. My mum's family brought together the Underhills and the Vincents both of whom appear to have had origins in rural Warwickshire and had moved into Birmingham in the mid-nineteenth century. Both the Vincents and Underhills at some stage had been involved in the jewellery trade and one of my forebears had risen to be a Master Jeweller. By the time I was born we had relatives in various parts of the city including Rednal, Longbridge and Bournville, but the centre of gravity for both families was in Handsworth and surrounding areas.

My paternal grandparents lived just off the City Road in a large terraced house, number 72, Cavendish Road. I remember the front door with its stained glass and the long pattern tiled floored hallway which went back to the kitchen which was reached down steps. There were two good sized rooms off the hall. There were two floors above this including the attic. I visited the road recently and it is little changed in appearance. In my memory the inside of the house was dark. It was the last in the terrace and abutted a green corrugated iron chapel of some kind so access to light may have been limited. Or perhaps my memory is simply faulty or has been shaped by a particular sequence of overcast days. One of my uncles still lived at home at this time while another was away doing his national service. Uncle Malcolm was the youngest brother in the family and was still a boy when I was a small child. As a consequence it was not unnatural that I spent more time with him when we visited and that I developed an element of hero worship for this older, bigger and stronger lad.

To get to Cavendish Road we travelled by bus first to Selly Oak and then on the outer circle route. At a very early age, perhaps three, I was carrying a much loved teddy bear which was left on the bus. I was distraught. We visited the City Road police station to see if it had been handed in. It had not. The sympathetic policeman on desk duty gave me a replacement bear that had been handed in. What I had not appreciated at the time was that while the loss of the toy was significant to me, far more significant to my father was the fact that the bear had been decorated with his own military medals.

On one visit while mum and dad talked in the sitting room with my grandparents and my father's older brother, Uncle Ray, and his wife, Auntie Sis, I spent time in the front room with my cousin Keith. Keith was a few months older than me and tended to take the lead. He decided it would be a good idea if we got granddad's record collection out to have a look at it. Unfortunately as he lifted a pile out he dropped them. In those days 78rpm records were very fragile and a large number of them broke. Keith's father responded with a prompt administration of corporal punishment. For some reason I got away scot free on this occasion.

I have warm memories of all my grandparents. Granddad Traves was a quiet man, below average height and with white hair. He was though very spritely for his age and had played football into his fifties. During his life I knew little of his background. In recent years an uncle told me that my granddad had been born to a relatively well-to-do family, his father being a clerk and later chief clerk to a Wolverhampton company. Granddad went to the prestigious St Peter's School and then on to university to study medicine with the intention of becoming a doctor. However, after a year his father went bankrupt, family legend says as a result of drink, and he could no longer afford to support my granddad at university. So granddad left and it was perhaps with the intention of at least pursuing some continuing interest in medicine that around 1912 he joined the army serving as a medical orderly.

He was a member of the Old Contemptibles, the first small British Expeditionary Force that went out to France in the Autumn of 1914. He saw action at Mons and Ypres among other battles. He spoke very little about the war but I did learn that he had lost part of an ear through frost bite and had a tooth taken out with a spoon without anaesthetic by a comrade. Dad told me that granddad had been captured towards the end of the rapid German advance in the Spring of 1918 but that in the muddle of the counter-offensive and the rapid withdrawal of the German army he and a friend had escaped. Sitting now on my window sill, kindly framed by my son

David, is the diploma he received in recognition of being mentioned in dispatches for gallantry. He was cited for going out under enemy fire to rescue injured soldiers in no-man's land.

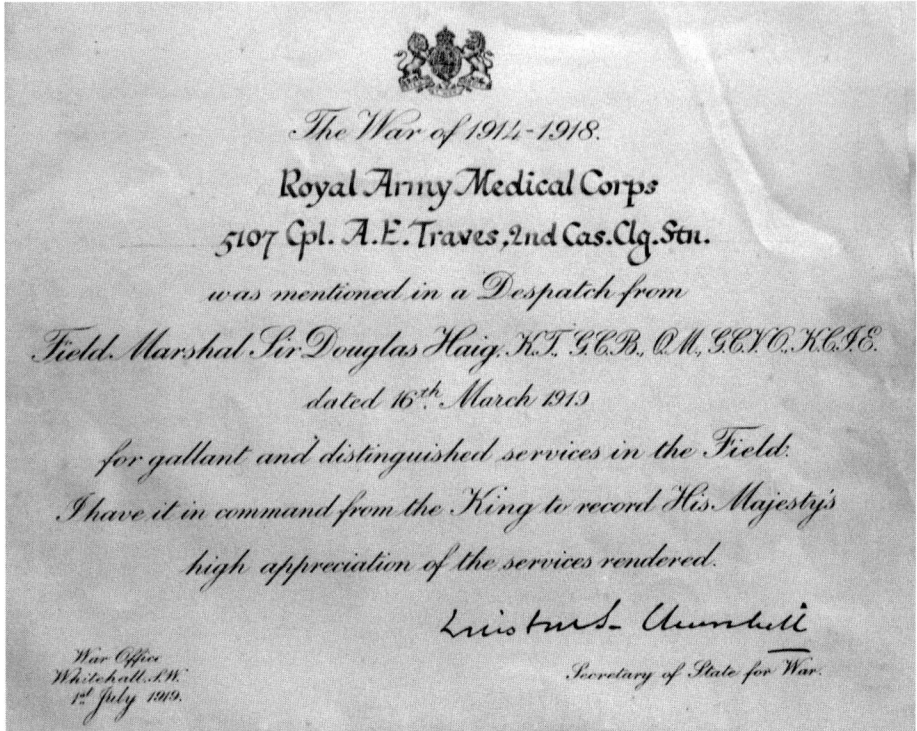

Certificate signed by Winston Churchill.

After the First World War he worked as one of the first generation of male nurses mainly in, what were then called, Lunatic Asylums. On retirement he ran for a while a mobile canteen that served a factory. Later he and my grandma moved down to Brixham in Devon where he died a few years later of lung cancer. Like so many of that generation he had experienced the most terrible events but, whatever mental scars he may have borne as a result, he carried on his life with a quiet determination and dignity.

Grandma Traves had a reputation for being tough, not to say hard. I never experienced this as she was always gentle with me and the general view is that I was a favourite with her. Born to a mining family in County Durham she became a nurse. She once told me that very early in her career she was based at Morpeth. A relative of a dead woman had come in one winter's evening to collect her personal effects and it was discovered that a ring had been left on the body. The sister instructed my grandmother, then no more than a girl of 16, to go across to the mortuary in the dark to take the ring from the dead woman's finger and bring it back.

– Weren't you afraid, Grandma?

– No lad. It's the living not the dead you've to fear.

Although not religious herself, the legacy of a northern Protestant upbringing lingered in her attitude to Catholicism and Catholics, all of whom she seemed to regard as adherents of the Whore of Babylon. On issues such as capital punishment my grandma's opinion was probably represented by the often repeated phrase about murderers that "hanging's too good for 'em".

Left to right: Grandma Traves, Jesse Lilly (mum's friend and bridesmaid), Uncle Ray, Dad, Mum, Auntie Den, Auntie Joan, Granddad Underhill, Grandma Underhill.

She met and married my granddad when she moved to the Midlands to get work and both of them served at one time between the wars in Dudley Road Hospital. After my grandfather's death I often went to stay with her in Brixham where I listened to her talking of her northern childhood. On her wall was an embroidered picture of her much loved Durham Cathedral. I think she would have been delighted to know that this is now my favourite building and that I would place it ahead of any of the great cathedrals of France or Italy in my affections.

Dad's oldest brother, Uncle Ray, was employed by the Gas Board like my dad. He was though sadly an ardent Birmingham City fan and this was a source of bewilderment to me as a convinced Villa supporter. Uncle was a teller of blue jokes. He never told these in front of me but he visited Fairway one time and stayed late long after I had been sent to bed. My mum the next morning was obviously still very much tickled by his jokes the night before;

Uncle Ray 1940s inscribed "To mum and dad from your loving son Ray".

– Ray was on form last night wasn't he. Mind you the one about the pole-vaulter was a bit close to the mark.

– About ten yards over it I would say.

I have pondered the various permutations for this joke ever since.

As boys my uncle and dad got into quite a few scrapes from what I heard. They were often in fights together. Uncle Stan, a younger brother, told me that when he was evacuated to the Worcestershire countryside in the war he had been very badly treated.

– Then your dad and Ray came to visit and had a word with the man of the family. After that they were really nice to me!

Uncle Ray's face and hands had a very rough and slightly pock-marked surface. I thought this a natural part of his appearance. Later again I learned the full story. Uncle had been a gunner in a bomber. The plane had crash-landed near Nottingham and burst into flames. Uncle Ray had pulled a fellow crew member out of the wreck but had been badly burned on the legs, face and hands as a result. On a later mission as a gunner in a Lancaster he had been machine gunned in the leg. Because the leg had already been skin grafted the wound would not heal properly. The surgeons advised Uncle Ray to have the leg amputated. He had refused. Throughout his life the leg was a source of great pain and was often ulcerated. On many occasions he said that he regretted he had not taken the surgeon's advice but he had been young he said, and what young man wants to lose a leg? In my early twenties I asked him about his experience as a rear gunner. What had it been like? I expected perhaps some bravado but there was none. You froze he said and for several hours you were cold and bored but with a growing sense of anxiety and fear the nearer you got to Germany. Then blinding fear.

– You know the expression, 'sh***ing yourself?' Well, there were times when it came very close to being literal.

He was contemptuous of the scenes in films where night fighters were shot down like fairground targets by rear gunners.

– You didn't see 'em. First thing you knew was you being shot at and then perhaps a plane moving across your vision before you had a chance to do anything. Most of the time you fired far too late to do any damage but it made you feel a bit better.

Uncle Geoff, one of my father's younger brothers, lived in Solihull. That in itself was enough to mark him out as the successful and wealthy member of the family. He was the only brother to have gone to grammar school, George Dixons on the City Road. He had set up his own business and done well. Getting across to Solihull meant getting a bus into town and then catching a Midland Red bus out to Solihull and then a walk round to my uncle's house which backed onto the grounds of a monastery. It was quite a lengthy and tiresome business getting across there but uncle sometimes generously fetched us and invariably ran us home. The house was new and well appointed with those symbols of affluence, fitted carpets, central heating and a new three piece suite. There was however nothing ostentatious about Uncle Geoff and Auntie Peggy. They had not been born to wealth but had worked hard for what they had. Auntie came from a family that owned a greengrocers in Hockley. Uncle was a fine cricketer and must have been close to county standard in his day. Cricket in the garden with uncle and my dad was the highlight of the visit as far as I was concerned.

The second youngest brother was Uncle Stan. My earliest memories are of him in uniform while doing his national service. Years later Stan, after telling me about some of the things my dad and Uncle Ray got up to was cajoled by his wife, Gina, to tell me about one his escapades as a child. When he was about 8 or 9 years old, still at primary school, he had been talking to a friend whose father had left the family and moved down to Bristol. The lad was determined to see his father and suggested to Stan that he join him in this adventure. Stan agreed.

– Get your mum to give you a few bob this lunchtime and meet me after school.

Stan succeeded in getting the money out of his mother;

– God knows what I told her to persuade her!

He duly met his mate at the school gate. The lad had borrowed a bike. Far too big for either of them but it was to be the mode of transport for the two hundred mile round trip. Stan climbed up behind his friend and they set off. Three days later they were resting still some miles short of their destination at the side of the road when a policeman rode past on his bike, looked intently at them, rode on a little, stopped, looked back and then returned. Stan and his mate had been blissfully unaware that their absence had of course raised a national alarm and their description had been sent out to police forces across the country. They were escorted to the police station and then placed in what Stan described as a really lovely large house in the country.

So lovely was the house and the treatment they received there that they were somewhat reluctant to return home with granddad who had travelled down to fetch them. Stan may also have been contemplating the kind of reception he might have expected from his mother. The idea of two primary school children travelling on one bike from Birmingham to Bristol has a kind of heroic quality about it although of course it is not a venture to be recommended. It is the kind of thing you can imagine the heroes of children's literature in the 1950s undertaking.

Grandma Traves had a number of sisters, all of whom went into nursing. One of them, Auntie Ethel, lived on the Bournville estate. She had risen to be a matron and was the epitome of what might have been presented as the image of the highly efficient, authoritative and rather fearsome figure of the archetypal matron. Everything about Auntie was neat and orderly from her appearance and dress to the decor of her house and garden. Every item had its place and was kept in its place. She was rather stern of appearance though very fond of my mum. Like my grandmother she retained the Durham accent and talked occasionally of the northern branch of the family with the famously tightfisted Uncle Tot and his equally prudent son Wilfred who had become an accountant. I stayed occasionally at Auntie Ethel's. The orderliness of the rooms was in stark contrast to the clean but disordered house at Fairway. In the morning at breakfast tea was served in a china teapot, jam was in a china pot with its own cover and a spoon that fitted in it, toast was brought to table in a toast rack, and, most impressive of all, a boiled egg was served with a little woollen cap to keep it hot. Later Auntie Ethel would join my grandma and another sister in the move to Brixham in Devon. Here she lavished extravagant affection on a poodle, much to the amazement of all her family. I had always seen Auntie Ethel as very much a single woman and I could not imagine her in a relationship with a man. Her views on men were not in general flattering and she credited very few of them with having any common-sense at all. Recently I learned that she had in fact been engaged as a young woman and that her fiancé was killed in the First World War. She will have been one of many women who experienced such loss and she will not have been unique in not forming another romantic relationship in her life.

Grandma's older sister was Betty. I knew little of her although she visited us on a couple of occasions. In her youth she had been courted up in County Durham by a young man called Tom who was a few years older than her. He had planned to emigrate and asked her to go with him. Whether her more conservatively minded family disapproved of this adventurous young man, whether she simply lacked the confidence for such a bold step or whether family ties were too strong, I don't know, but despite her love for him she did not go. Tom went off alone. Betty remained single. Years later when they were both elderly he contacted her. He had become a wealthy businessman and was now a widower living out in Australia. He had never forgotten Betty and asked her to join him. He came back to England and they married. They had only a few years together, living I think out in Australia, before Tom died. I met him once when he visited our house. His life story was like something out of a Jack London novel. He had been in a gold rush as a prospector. He had worked on ranches in Australia and he gave a vivid account of a shark attack in an Australian estuary in which a man had lost his legs. All this seemed very romantic and exotic even when told beside the fire of a suburban house in Northfield.

Often when visiting my paternal grandparents we would take the opportunity to visit mum's aunt, Edie. Auntie Edie was the sister of my maternal granddad. She lived alone, for she had never married, in rented rooms on the ground floor of an enormous house on City Road. The house was even darker in my memory than Cavendish Road and it had a strange rather musty smell. Auntie Edie was a gentle soul who was extremely fond of my mum. On visits I was allowed to play in the garden and even to venture through the rear gate into Summerfield Park. I am afraid to say that much as I liked Auntie Edie, I found these visits dull, especially when my mother made a special trip to go there and we would spend all day at City Road. These trips usually included an outing to go shopping on the Dudley Road which did not add to their attraction for me. Though the visits were dull there were mysteries about Auntie Edie's house. There were people called lodgers. One of whom, a woman of about the same age as Auntie, occupied the front room. I rarely met this woman but I think my mother told me that she was Jewish; my first experience of meeting or even being aware of someone from a different cultural background.

My Aunt also used to be very active as a volunteer at something she called, "The Settlement". She talked to mum a great deal about this and it was clearly at the centre of her social life. It meant nothing to me then and I thought little about it in later years. It was only while writing this that I bothered to look up the Birmingham Settlement which was the most likely settlement that Auntie Edie was involved with. When I read about it I felt a deep sense of sadness that I had so under-estimated this kind, gentle and unpretentious woman. The Settlement, part of the wider movement influenced by the historian T.H. Green and by Arthur Toynbee, was founded in 1899 by a group of wealthy female philanthropists. Its work focused initially almost exclusively on women and was staffed by female residents and volunteers and worked to alleviate the impact of poverty and to increase the life chances and choices of the poor and the excluded. The Settlement offered, among other things, a savings scheme, infant welfare clinics, free legal advice and a recreational club that included a temperance pub. It campaigned for the rights of divorced women to obtain maintenance, provided a hostel for homeless women and care services

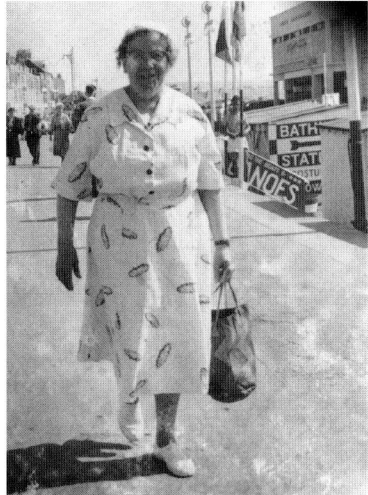

Auntie Edie – 1950s.

for the elderly. All this must have been vital to the poor and the vulnerable in an age that was harsher and where the state provided so little. It still does outstanding work to this day. This has been a reminder to me of the dangers of shallow judgement and of a goodness and generosity that made no claims for itself, that was not perhaps based in a political ideology but in a genuine and profound decency. I wish I had known more of this and been able to talk to her about it and to have demonstrated some level of recognition of her altruism. It is over fifty years too late to do this now.

Travelling by Midland Red bus was a more exotic form of transport. These buses were slightly smarter than the Birmingham Corporation yellow and blue buses and they were more expensive. The conductors delivered printed paper tickets rather than the small rectangular stiffer tickets issued on Birmingham buses. All of these things marked them out for me as distinctive. But the key difference was that these buses travelled to more distant places: Worcester, Leamington, Droitwich, Redditch and beyond. It was by Midland Red that my mother and I would make our rare visits to Auntie Ada. Auntie Ada was my maternal grandfather's oldest sister. She lived in a large rather decaying property in an inner suburb of Coventry. Auntie Ada was a friendly woman but more austere in appearance than her sister Edie. While Edie was dark of complexion and even still dark of hair, Ada was light of complexion with white hair drawn back sharply into a single bun at the back.

Coventry was another country as far as I was concerned and I had no idea just how close it really was to Birmingham. The feel of the place was different, the accent different and the centre was almost entirely brand new. I learned early on that this was the result of the terrible bombing raid on Coventry. My grandparents had told me that on that November night in 1940 you could see from their home in Rednal the glow in the sky of the inferno in Coventry. Auntie Ada's house was Victorian. It was on several floors and stood on the corner of a street. Parts of the house, like Auntie Edie's, were let out to lodgers, none of whom I ever met. The house was large and dark and had a lingering smell of damp. The garden was long with a stream running through it. Everything, including my aunt, seemed to have seen better days. Auntie Ada had inherited the house from her husband who was considerably older than her. She had married late in life after caring for him as his housekeeper for many years. She had been engaged in her youth but her fiancé, having survived the First World War, died in the great influenza epidemic of 1919.

Mum's family, on both sides, had settled first in the centre of Birmingham near or in the Jewellery Quarter. By the time of the

First World War most of them had moved out to Handsworth or areas nearby. My great-grandmother's home had been in Uplands Road, just off the Soho Road. The house had eventually been inherited by Auntie Nell, grandma's younger sister. It was a small terraced house of the back-to-back variety common in that area and a feature of the expansion of cities in the nineteenth century. Auntie Nell was by the time I knew her well into her middle age, to me she appeared positively elderly though she would only have been in her late forties at most. People, particularly working class people, appeared older sooner in those days. I have photos of my grandma at the time she married in her early twenties and she was a beautiful young woman. Ten years later looking decidedly middle-aged, heavy set and with false teeth, she dressed and wore her hair in the manner of the older generation. Auntie Nell was married to a very odd character, Uncle Fred. Fred was from the potteries and spoke with an accent that I found almost incomprehensible. He was a little man with thick glasses. He had a car, a Standard. When we visited he would often offer to run us home. I always wondered why my parents desperately looked for excuses not to take up the offer. After all the journey back involved at least two buses and on winter evenings a cold wait at bus stops. The reason was Uncle Fred's driving. Or rather the team effort of Auntie Nell and Uncle Fred. Auntie Nell had never learned to drive but Fred could not undertake any journey without her beside him to share in all decisions, when to turn, when to pull out, when to brake, when to change gear. Whether or not it was his poor eyesight but any attempt to cross traffic was always fraught with the greatest danger. Auntie Nell assumed complete responsibility for traffic observation to the left;

– Not yet Fred.

– All clear.

Her judgement was shaky, but his was dire. The fault lay according to him and his co-driver, however, not with his poor eyesight, lack of basic driving skills or non-existent road sense, but with the fact that the roads were full of "maniacs". The definition of a "maniac" appeared to be anyone who had the audacity to be coming towards them at a time when they wanted to cross traffic or who thought it reasonable to travel more than 25 miles an hour on an open road. My father who had nerves of steel invariably arrived home shaken after such journeys.

Auntie Nell's story, however, was a sad one. As a young woman she had an affair with a married man and became pregnant. In the 1930s this would have been regarded as a real disgrace in a respectable working class family. Her family, however, was a loving one and the offer was made by her older sister, my grandmother, to adopt the baby at birth. I suspect Auntie Nell came under considerable moral pressure from the family to agree to this and so it came to pass. Joan, her daughter, was brought up as the child of my grandparents. She was deeply loved in that family, perhaps even spoiled by her older sisters and her devoted adopted parents. It was not until Joan was in her late teens and wanted to go abroad and thus required a passport and needed her birth certificate that grandma and granddad felt compelled to tell her the truth about her parentage. Auntie Nell longed for Joan to acknowledge her as her mother and to call her by that name. Joan could not do so. To her, her adopted parents were real parents in everything but biological fact. It was a source of deep pain and sadness to Auntie Nell to her dying day.

Living close to Auntie Nell was her sister, Auntie Lil. Like my grandparents, Auntie Lil lived in a terraced 1920s council house. She was a quietly spoken and kind woman who had had a hard life in earlier years married to a difficult man. One of my early memories is of visiting him in a sanatorium on the edge of Birmingham, at Romsley. TB was a great scourge in those days and these sanatoriums were full of sufferers. They were often designed, as was the case at this hospital, with the potential to open the wards up to the outside air, with the idea that the bracing wind would help heal or at least ease the diseased lungs. Whatever the scientific basis of this theory it did not work for Auntie Lil's husband and he died in the mid-1950s and in some ways it must have been a release for my aunt as her life with him had been an unhappy one. Auntie Lil was for many years alone but later through work she met a thoroughly decent man, Len, who made her very happy. It was a happiness she thoroughly deserved.

Auntie Lil had three children, Don, Roy and Sheila. The children all inherited her inner strength and kindness. Sheila was deserted by her husband and left to bring up five young children on her own. She did so with great success. Don lost his wife at a very early age to cancer and he too did a remarkable job raising his children alone. Roy, the eldest joined the police and married a young Irish nurse, Phil. Phil was vivacious, witty and lovely. They are still a devoted couple after almost sixty years of marriage and Phil still as funny, irreverent and charming as ever.

Close by Auntie Nell and Lil was mum's sister, Denise. Married to a policeman, Fred, Auntie later became a long-serving and much loved teaching assistant at a nearby primary school. Auntie Den had two daughters, Jackie and Gill. Tragically, Jackie, an immensely clever and gifted woman who was also extraordinarily pleasant, died in her early forties of cancer. Gill has become very much a key figure in the extended family over recent decades. I think Auntie Den's daughters were given the share of common-sense and practical ability that I so clearly lack!

While we made regular visits across to Handsworth to visit my mum's aunts and younger sister Denise, it was with Auntie Rhona, the sister closest in age to my mother, that we had greatest contact. We made a visit to Farren Road at least once a week and Auntie Rhona and her two children, and later three, came down to us once a week as well. Farren Road linked the Bristol Road South and Tessall Lane in Longbridge and backed onto fields with the Austin factory beyond that. My mother and her sister were very close and Auntie Rhona's son, Ian became the inseparable friend of my brother Richard.

Auntie's husband, Uncle Tony was a unique figure in the family. He was universally liked but seen as somewhat eccentric. This came in part from the fact that he was a voracious reader and would not only always have a book to hand but usually found it difficult to resist getting involved in it even on family social occasions. Uncle had lost the hearing in one ear due to an infection in his teens. This made it hard for him to hear from that side though I suspect he sometimes favoured the deaf ear to avoid unwanted interruption to his reading.

The two families spent a number of holidays together camping or staying in caravans. Uncle had bought a Landrover one year but on the way down towards a west country holiday it broke down with a holed radiator. Undaunted dad and Uncle Tony pulled into a field and while the two women brewed up and prepared some food they drove off in dad's car to locate a new radiator. In the meantime Auntie Rhona and mum removed the radiator and the two men fitted the new one and we continued on our way. Uncle was also a great admirer of Scotland and visited with his family as often as possible and though he could find no ancestral roots there, he clearly felt a great affinity with the landscape, people and culture. It was on the Woolacombe Bay holiday that uncle decided to wear the kilt he had bought. This attracted much attention and the gentle mockery of dad who to the delight of all except my uncle, rolled up his trousers, wrapped himself in a tartan rug and wore a transistor radio as a sporran to accompany Uncle Tony. Uncle was a good enough sport not to be offended.

One afternoon in 1961 at Farren Road dad and Uncle Tony were earnestly consulting a book. My uncle was quoting page numbers to my father. They would then study these pages together. I had no idea what was going on but I did note the title, which at the time meant nothing to me. It was *Lady Chatterley's Lover* and it had of course been the subject of a famous trial the previous autumn. No doubt my uncle was informing my dad of the pages with the greatest literary merit!

Uncle Tony was in fact a remarkable man. Brought up in Quinton by his working class parents, Tony, an only child had been deeply loved. Though not wealthy the family had an interesting background and one of his uncles, Dick, had been a life-long socialist and had in his old age studied law. Self-education was a strong tradition in the Sabell family and uncle was clearly deeply influenced by this. He went to Five Ways grammar school but did not go on to university despite his obvious intelligence. I would guess that the expense would have been too great. Instead he went to train as an optician at Scriveners. Over the years uncle established an international reputation for his knowledge of the newly emerging field of contact lenses. He would go on to become a senior lecturer at Aston University and even in his late seventies his work as a consultant at Queen Elizabeth Hospital was highly regarded. A few years before his death he was deservedly awarded the OBE.

Uncle also took a profound interest in the history and literature of the First World War and his collection of medals associated with nursing and medicine, was regarded as one of the finest of its kind. Uncle always took a kindly interest in me and was, I think, pleased that I also was a reader with an interest in history. He gave me some of the most treasured of my presents as a lad, a wonderful medieval castle that he had crafted for me and later a three volume Victorian set of books entitled, *The World's Greatest Paintings*. A few weeks before his death I visited him and was talking to him about Pat Barker's First World War trilogy, *Regeneration*. He pondered for a while and then disappeared upstairs. When he came back down he had his annotated copies of Siegfried Sassoon's diaries and a series of original articles about Dr Rivers, a central character in Barker's novels. After his death Auntie said that he had left these books especially for me and that I could have a pick of any others I chose. I was greatly moved by this.

If Handsworth was the nearest a family like mine got to an ancestral home and Fairway was the focus of the nuclear family, it was 223 Cliff Rock Road Rednal that was the hub for the extended family, the home of my maternal grandparents.

The family gathered at Cliff Rock Road for key events and celebrations such as Christmas afternoon. During that time representatives from the wider Vincent and Underhill families would drop in, Auntie Hilda, grandma's sister-in-law, Uncle Ron her youngest brother who would come down from Ruskington in Lincolnshire, Barry, Hilda's son, great aunts Edie and Ada, Sheila, Don or Roy, grandma's nieces and nephews. There was only the one living room downstairs so I wonder how we all fitted in, but I never remember any sense of it being over-crowded anymore than I remember people not being welcomed.

My grandparents had moved to, what were then, brand new council houses on the very edge of Birmingham in the 1920s. They had moved from rented rooms in Laxey Road, just off the City Road near Summerfield Park. As the years went on new private and council house development swept up the hill from the Bristol Road so that by the time I came along the terraced house was part of an extensive mixed housing estate.

My Aunt Joan still lived at home for much of my childhood and adolescence. She was to me a figure of considerable glamour. Joan, who worked at the University of Birmingham as a lab assistant, had expensive tastes by the standards of the family. She shopped from time to time at the up-market store Marshall and Snelgrove's on New Street and later at Rackham's on Corporation Street which had been owned by Harrods and shared some of that brand's prestige. She also had a collection of records including one I remember very vividly, it was Kathleen Ferrier singing, "Blow the Winds Southerly", probably the first time I came across a world class operatic voice. Joan accompanied my family on a number of holidays including the extended drive across Europe through Austria and on to northern Italy in the mid-sixties.

Birthday and Christmas presents from Joan were always a particular delight as they were carefully chosen and often quite expensive. One year, when I was about eight or nine, Joan's birthday treat was a surprise visit to London. We awoke very early to get a coach from Digbeth Station. In London we visited Madame Tussaud's, the Tower, and Westminster and had fish and chips at

Lyons Corner House, Trafalgar Square. As the day went on I felt more and more lethargic and sick and eventually disgorged the entire Lyons House meal. Mum was greatly annoyed that I failed to respond positively to what was clearly a wonderful gift. She was thoroughly penitent the next day when I was diagnosed with chicken pox.

*Mum with two of her sisters and children
circa 1960. Back row: Jackie, Richard, Ian.
Front row: Auntie Den, Gill, Auntie Rhona, Triona, Mum.*

Grandma and granddad enjoyed one of the happiest of marriages. Their deep affection for each other did not dim across the years and granddad's death at the age of 69 was a source of deepest grief for my grandmother. They had met before the First World War when my grandma was working in a shop in the Jewellery Quarter and my granddad was the local post boy, riding his bike past the shop and clearly making his admiration evident. He was a handsome young man and she a very beautiful young woman and they must have made an impressive couple. At 16 my grandfather lied about his age and joined the Royal Horse Artillery. His mother went straight to the recruiting office to set them straight about his actual age but to no avail and off to France he went. In 1917 when the Austrians broke through in northern Italy at Caporetto, he was sent as part of the Franco-British reinforcement out there. It was in the Italian campaign that he was injured by shrapnel. He returned to Britain for treatment and then went back out to France just as the war ended. Like granddad Traves, granddad Underhill did not talk about his wartime experiences.

They married in the early 1920s and soon settled in Cliff Rock Road. They had three daughters and later adopted Joan who was never less than a full daughter to them. Grandma gave up work when she had children. Granddad was not highly paid but work with the post office was secure. He took his work very seriously and felt that the delivery of mail was an enormously worthwhile job. At that time there was of course no internet and few houses had private phones. The regular delivery of letters was, therefore, the main means by which people kept in contact with each other. It was possible before the Second World War to post a letter in the morning and have it delivered in the afternoon. There were Christmas Day deliveries in those days and one year granddad rose very early on the 25th December to find that there was deep snow and buses and trams were not running. The idea of not delivering on that day of all days was anathema to him so he walked the nine or so miles from Rednal to the city centre to make sure he could carry out his delivery. He rose from postman to inspector and I have an early memory of being taken one Christmas to the sorting office in Victoria Square to be made much of by his work-mates. I still treasure the watch he received

Granddad and Grandma Underhill and me – 1950.

from his colleagues on his retirement in 1957 and which was passed on to me by grandma after his death.

After mum's death my wife and I were helping clear her house. We discovered an album of cards sent between my grandma and granddad during and immediately after the First World War. They are a tender testament to their affection and to the deep anxieties they must have felt during the war. When writing on the eve of his return to France, "May God protect you and keep you safe to return to me" this was no empty set of words from my grandmother but a profoundly held hope and prayer.

Grandma survived her husband by over ten years but she missed him greatly. On returning from the local library with her one day she told me

Granddad Underhill, Cliff Rock Road late 1950s.

that when Albert was alive and she went out shopping she would see him on her return in the window watching out for her. She said she knew now that he would not of course be framed in the windows as she turned up from Leach Green Road into Cliff Rock Road but still somewhere there was the lingering hope that he would be and the profound sadness that he was not.

Grandma Underhill, mum and me, Cliff Rock Road 1951.

As she lay close to death grandma asked to hold the precious letters he had sent her on her wedding day over sixty years before. The first was addressed to Miss Phyllis Vincent and was received by her on the morning of the wedding at her parents' address. The second addressed to Mrs Phyllis Underhill was received by her when they arrived at their new marital home after the ceremony. My grandfather was a quiet and modest man not given to outpourings of sentiment. This romantic gesture and these short but deeply touching letters are a tribute to his love for his new wife, a love that endured to the end of his life.

Cliff Rock Road 2016.

13

The box in the corner

– Now?
– No.
– And now?
– Nothing.
– Now?
– Better. Yes that's it... No... Gone again.

MY DAD is up in the loft. We are down in the living room. He is adjusting the aerial while we relay commentary on whether or not a picture is emerging. We had tried the set top aerial that came with the TV but that had been a miserable failure. The only places where there was any hint of a picture would have meant someone standing on a chair with the aerial held aloft. So it was the aerial in the loft option and eventually a position was found that provided reasonable reception. It is 1960 and we have joined the TV owning population.

The development of television and television viewing was a significant feature of life in the 1950s and early 1960s. In 1950, the year of my birth, TVs were very expensive, the equivalent of several months income for people like my parents. TV ownership was therefore still relatively rare though growing. The sets had tiny screens, often no more than 9 inches in diameter, set in wooden cabinets. Until 1955 there was only one channel, the BBC. The advent of ITV, a commercial channel, was controversial and highly exciting. We would now be spoiled for choice with two options each night. Access to TV was further restricted in terms of time. The network closed down each night and there were times during the day when it was closed, in the early evening for example to allow parents time to put their children to bed. Between each programme a formally dressed and Oxbridge accented presenter would introduce the next programme.

Breakdowns were commonplace both in terms of the network and the set. When the transmission failed a test card came up with the announcement that "Normal service will be resumed as soon as possible". Sets tended to lose vertical or horizontal hold which led to the picture spinning either down the screen or across it. The viewer then had to adjust the hold knobs. This led to the frustration that if you went a fraction too far the picture began to spin in the opposite direction. Like car driving in those days TV viewing was fraught with the constant threat of a breakdown of some kind but we accepted this as a normal if occasionally frustrating occurrence. This is what we had bought into and it was a source of great excitement to the family. Even the aerial adjustment was an event in its own right.

We had not owned a set up to this point so my viewing had taken place on visits to relatives or others who had a TV. Principle among these were my grandparents' neighbours, Mr and Mrs Maddox in Cliff Rock Road. Mr Maddox worked at the Austin car factory and was I guess well paid by the standards of the time. In any event they had a TV and I was often invited, or invited myself, around to watch. What I remember most vividly from this early period are the adventure series like *The Sword of Freedom* and *Ivanhoe*. But topping them all was the weekly *Robin Hood* starring Richard Green. I would be utterly engrossed from the first notes of its introductory theme song;

"Robin Hood, Robin Hood riding through the glen...
Robin Hood, Robin Hood with his band of men,

Feared by the bad, loved by the good,
Robin Hood, Robin Hood, Robin Hood."

It was a pretty sanitised version of the story with no grubby peasants, no Nottingham Streets full of offal and no gruesome punishments held in public. Robin and his men, despite living in a forest with no obvious access to a laundry were always immaculately turned out in their neatly ironed green suits. Maid Marion clearly knew of some peasant hovel in the vicinity where her make-up could be faultlessly applied. Each week the formula was pretty much the same. Robin and his men would respond to some injustice on the part of the wicked Sheriff of Nottingham, get into a tight corner and finally escape triumphant from danger to the chagrin or humiliation of the villain. Each time I saw it, however, the tension proved too much and I would hide behind the settee until the danger passed.

Early popular series for children included *Davy Crockett* and the cartoon *Popeye*. Popeye with his Bronx accent, habitual pipe and misshapen arms tattooed with an anchor, spent most of each episode being bullied and tortured by his arch enemy the enormous and bearded Bluto, while Popeye's girlfriend Olive Oil spent most of the episode screaming for help as Bluto carried her off. But all came well in the end each time as Popeye, about to be crushed, roasted or otherwise annihilated succeeded in opening a tin of spinach and swallowing it. This instantly transformed him into a cartoon super-hero and led to the complete destruction of Bluto. Popeye also generated, among us children, songs parodying the theme tune which may have lacked craft and sophistication but which we found extraordinarily witty and risqué. These were sung in our best Brummie version of a Bronx accent:

"I'm Popeye the sailor man
I live in a caravan
The girls are so doity
They pull up my shoity

I'm Popeye the sailor man.
Poop, poop!"

A criticism levelled at TV from some quarters was that it was a threat to family life. However, from my memory it was in fact treated largely as a family activity. Programmes were usually watched together and, certainly in my home, TV was never left on as a background noise; we were either watching or it was off. Furthermore, far from stifling conversation it was a source of discussion before, during and after. So what was it that we watched?

A staple of TV viewing then was the quiz show, many of them adapted versions of American shows. These shows had a number of attractions. They offered the chance for people recognisably like us to be on TV. Ordinary people plucked from an audience perhaps with a chance to win the kind of money or luxury items that would have required years of savings. They often combined the challenge of general knowledge questions with elements of a gentle ritual mockery.

Among the programmes we liked was *Take Your Pick* with Michael Miles. At the start of the programme the night's prizes were introduced to the audience. These ranged from the three absurd booby prizes, "a rusty nail", "a broken spring", "a pair of odd shoes", "last night's leftovers"...you get the idea, through to a set of kitchen knives, a decorative ashtray and the weekly Treasure Chest which might contain between ten and fifty pounds and on finally to the star prize as the curtain was opened to the impressed oooohhhh! from the audience as a television set, fridge, cooker or three piece suite was revealed and described. At this stage we would compare notes as a family as to which prizes we would most like to win. This could produce quite an extended and even vaguely surreal discussion with points earnestly raised for and against each chosen favourite;

– But where would we fit the wardrobe Beryl?
– We'd get rid of the chest of drawers in our bedroom Reg.

Each competitor had then to undergo the "Yes-No game" in which Michael Miles would question them at speed trying within a set time limit to get them to say one of the forbidden words: "Yes" or "No". If successful the competitor won the princely sum of ten bob, 50p in new money. It was designed as a warm up to the main act and as a source of amusement as competitors got increasingly tangled up in their answers.

– You didn't say "yes" then did you?

– No.

Bong!

The main game involved answering a series of general knowledge questions correctly which gave the competitor the chance to choose the key to one of ten boxes. There was an additional Box 13 but that will just complicate matters. Each locked box contained a card that corresponded to one of the prizes. Having successfully answered the questions the competitor was choosing blind. The prize behind the locked door might be a three piece suite or a rusty nail.

– And remember viewers even I don't know what is in the boxes.

At this point, the competitor having made the choice, Michael Miles begins to offer cash for the key. He takes cash out and begins to lay it on top of the boxes.

Five pounds for the key, c'mon Bob that's £5... five crisp pound notes.

He counts the notes out on top of the mystery boxes.

– OK Bob. Ten pounds? Twenty?

He might go higher or he might stop at five. The audience, with our unheard contributions from home, yells;

– Take the money!

or

– Open the box!

The competitor turns down the money and opens the box. Michael Miles with great drama opens the box and holding the card away from the competitor says;

– So Bob, you turned down £25.

Dramatic pause.

– You turned down £25 and you have won...

Pause...

– A rusty nail!

Groans from the audience and probably an internal expletive from Bob who earns less than £10 a week.

– But never mind Bob, you've been a great sport. Give him a big hand folks!

Of course it might be an alternative scenario. Bob is tempted by the certainty of several weeks wages and takes the £25. The box is opened.

– Bob you took the £25. It's now in your pocket. Bob, you would have won...

pause...

– Tonight's star prize, the fridge!

More groans from the audience and Bob goes home to a disappointed wife denied the luxury fridge. At home we are divided between those who are vindicated in the unheard advice we shouted at the screen and those feeling complicit in persuading poor Bob to the wrong decision. Quiz shows also had the added bonus of being able to test and at times flaunt your own general knowledge and feel smug at the expense of the ignorant contestant who "didn't even know that..." Questions we couldn't answer were automatically designated by the family as "very hard".

The home produced programmes were supplemented by imports from the USA. Like GIs these all seemed bigger, brasher and more glamorous. US Westerns and detective series were particularly popular. Each week we watched *Wagon Train*, a series of adventures based around a wagon train on its journey westward. It was a testament to the resilience of the people making this journey as it clearly lasted for almost a decade and they had an adventure, crime, indian attack or tragedy each week. Ward Bond played the trustworthy, brave but grumpy wagon train leader as it made its way from post-Civil War Missouri towards California. I was allowed to stay up late to watch this as it finished after my official bedtime and it is the first of the major Western series I remember watching on a regular basis. Then there was *Rawhide*, starring the young and as yet unknown, Clint Eastwood, as the ramrod on the cattle drive, Rowdy Yates. Eastwood made his name in this series and established the tough, taciturn character for which he was to become famous. None of us of course had the least idea what a ramrod was. These were just two of the many Western series, others included, *Gun Smoke, Bronco, Bonanza* and *Maverick*. We were pretty avid Western viewers and most weeks we watched at least one of these series.

A particular favourite of ours was the American comic series *Bilko* starring Phil Silvers. Like the British series *The Army Game* it appealed to an audience of adults who had done National Service in one of the armed forces. Unlike many programmes from the past *Bilko* remains a comic masterpiece worthy of revisiting today, a tribute to the genius of Phil Silvers.

On Saturday evenings we watched whatever the current detective series was from America. These were so much glossier than homegrown programmes like *No Hiding Place* or the ultimately sedate, *Dixon of Dock Green*. The latter was a police series set in the traditional East End and was inspired by a very fine film, *The Blue Lamp*. Each week PC Dixon introduced the episode and each week he rounded off with a short homily. Towards the end of a run lasting over twenty years it became somewhat embarrassing as the ageing Jack Warner looked increasingly absurd as he sought to tackle the villains. What it did have however, was very good writing from Ted Willis and a setting in a working class environment that would have been recognisable and convincing to the millions who lived in similar communities.

The American series by contrast were glamorous and slick and the production values were in many ways far higher reflecting the much more generous budgets available. There was no sense of a community setting with the possible exception of the darkly urban, *Dragnet*. Others like *77 Sunset Strip* were set in an entirely exotic world where teenagers drove cars, every house had all the latest gadgets and where huge soft-top convertibles were parked by Cookie, a Fonz-like figure, who never opened the car door but always leapt over it.

One of the highlights of the television week was *Sunday Night at the London Palladium*. The hosts of the show changed over the years but included, Tommy Trinder, Bruce Forsyth, Norman Vaughan and Jimmy Tarbuck. The first half of the show included a range of acts, all or most of whom had at least a national reputation. The acts would be interspersed with jokes from the host or dancing from the famous Tiller Girls, high kicking and scantily dressed, a kind of sanitised version of the can-can as performed at the Moulin Rouge. The second half was dominated by the week's star and this included performers with major international reputations. Star billing included in 1957 Mario Lanza the opera singer turned film star a man widely adored by women and in 1963 The Beatles. Again I was allowed at times to stay up late to watch this programme.

In addition to the weekly highlights or regulars there were the annual events. These seemed to figure much larger in the calendar and in our imaginations than their equivalent today, though perhaps for some modern viewers the final of *The X Factor* or *Strictly Come Dancing* have a similar stature. Two stand out for me. *The Royal Variety Performance* was notable partly because of the build up, partly because of its length, in my memory it seemed to be on all evening. In the 1950s acts like Flanagan and Allen received an especially warm reception from the audience. As a young viewer I could not see what attracted people to two middle aged men, one of whom was in a fur coat, singing "Underneath the Arches". What I of course failed to realise was the depth of emotion evoked by acts and voices like Tommy Trinder, Flanagan and Allen and Vera Lynn that were so closely associated with the Second World War. Only as I got older did I begin to appreciate just how recent in the memories of adults the war was in the 1950s and 60s.

The star television event running up to Christmas was, for my dad and me at least, *Sports Personality of the Year*. Again it seemed to occupy the whole night not finishing until some unimaginable hour like 10pm and I was allowed to stop up to see the final announcement of the winner. The format was not dissimilar to the current programme but perhaps because choice and live sport was so much more limited it seemed to us a major event in the year, a milestone not to be missed. It produced, as it still does to some extent, the annual household arguments in favour or against the choices made.

Dad was interested in sport and so was I so we watched whatever was shown when we had the opportunity. The flagship BBC programme was *Grandstand*, one of the few I watched alone as dad worked on Saturdays. There was no live football but there were updates on scores and a wide range of other sports coverage including motorbike scrambling and horse racing. Then there were the annual major events. Top of the list for me was Cup Final Day. I would turn the TV on as soon as coverage started in the morning when there would be a summary of "the routes to the final" for both clubs and a brief review of the last decade of finals. This latter item delighted me because in that period it included of course the Villa win of 1957. This would be followed by an introduction to the teams then a build up with the crowd joining in the hymn, *Abide With Me* and then full coverage of the game. Some years I watched with my fellow Villa supporting cousin Robert. On these occasions the match was followed by the two of us replaying it outside in the road with a tennis ball. For some obscure reason we accompanied our play with commentary each taking over as we had the ball;

– Vincent moving forward now, displaying the skills that have made him such a favourite with the crowds up and down the land.

– But he is tackled by Traves who once again puts on the burst of dazzling speed that makes him so feared by defenders...

However, if I had to pick one defining sporting TV event from these years it would have to be, without question, the World Cup of 1966. Each match was watched. Each match discussed at length at home and school. Having played out a dull opening draw England made their way through the group stage to play the designated villains of the competition, Argentina. On past that round, courtesy of the sending off of the Argentine captain. "What could you expect?" was the tone from BBC commentator Kenneth Wolstenholm as he passed judgement on the foul. And thus the clean cut Englishmen disposed of the shady South Americans. On to Portugal with the dazzling Eusebio. Victory and a place in the final against West Germany.

What was remarkable, and it happened again in the 2012 Olympics, was that people who never took the slightest interest in sport were transformed over the weeks of the cup into avid fans. Mum was such a person. I am not certain she was entirely sure on the offside rule; in fact, given the questions and comments she made during matches I'm not convinced she was sure on virtually any of the rules or conventions of the game. However, come the Saturday of the final she was utterly committed as an England supporter and as nervous as anyone else.

A tense opening and then disaster as West Germany opened the scoring. Gloomy predictions around the room. Then delight and the restoration of optimism as Hurst equalises and then delirious joy as Peters put us ahead. Minutes only to go. The door bell rings. Magnanimously I offer to open it. It's the milkman come to be paid. As he returns the change he asks;

– How's it going?

– We've won ...good as.

As I return to the room mum is furious with me.

– You shouldn't say that, it's tempting fate. They'll score now.

And as we all know, they did.

– I told you, I told you about saying that. Now look what's happened.

I genuinely felt guilty as if there really was a connection between what I had said to the Midland Dairies milkman and the late German goal. All turned out well. Fate decided that my hubris had been adequately punished and after the dodgy third goal and the "some people think it's all over, well it is now" fourth, we raised the Jules Rimet trophy, described by Wolstenholm as;

"It's only twelve inches high but it means that England are the World Champions."

Bobby Moore holds the trophy aloft, Wembley 1966.

The world order of football appeared to all English men and women to have been restored. The first of many we thought. Still waiting.

TV, as it still does, excited much popular debate about its potential impact on family life, culture, reading, concentration spans and the health of our eyes. The 1950s was a far more paternalistic age than the present. Educated men in positions of authority felt it was their moral and social responsibility to protect the unwashed poor like us from the corrupting influence of mass entertainment. It was thus more common then for some pundits, like Malcolm Muggeridge, to lament the vulgarisation of cultural life that was seen as the direct result of the rapid growth in TV viewing. Individual programmes stimulated lively arguments about their value. The general rule appeared to be that the more popular a programme was the more damaging and low brow it must be, and if added to its popularity, it was AMERICAN, well say no more.

I would be more persuaded by the merits of these arguments if it could be shown that prior to television the average family gathered regularly to read and discuss George Eliot or went in droves to hear Mozart's *Requiem*. Of course, as now, we often complained that there was "nothing worth watching tonight" or that particular programmes were rubbish or even, as my dad might add, "American rubbish". Some of the productions were shoddy and appear amateurish today. There was a great deal of patronisation of ordinary people as there still is. However, television occasionally introduced to me as a lad from a very ordinary home, a world of culture I would

had but that was when he was posted to Palestine in 1948 with the army. I understood therefore that it was simply not feasible.

Two days later mum and dad told me that they had thought about it and decided that they would find the money, that this was too good an opportunity to be missed for me. It could be paid in weekly instalments and they would manage. The consent form was duly signed and I returned it to Mr Heseltine, my English teacher and the organiser of the trip only be told that unfortunately it was now full. That seemed to be that. Then a couple of days later Mr Heseltine asked to see me. Someone had dropped out of the trip and noting how disappointed I had looked he was offering that place to me on condition that I returned the consent form and deposit the following day. I did. I was going to Venice.

It is hard now to imagine just how exotic a foreign trip appeared to ordinary people in 1962. Cheap package tours were about to be launched on a large scale but as yet foreign holidays were a real rarity. Few members of my family on my father or mother's side had gone abroad for a holiday. The wars and national service represented for some of the males in the family the only experience of other countries. I knew nothing about Venice except that it had canals. I knew even less about Italy except that it was where the Romans had come from. You have to add to this lack of experience of travel an almost total absence on British menus of the time of foreign food. I genuinely believed that spaghetti was something sold in a can by Heinz and served in a tomato sauce very similar to that found in baked beans. So foreign countries really were "foreign": strange and exotic.

The trip organiser, Mr Heseltine, was a real character. He was Jewish and was at times the subject of foul anti-semitic comments behind his back, a reminder of how deep and how open anti-semitism was at the time. He taught a range of subjects including English and Maths. He was in the category of sound but dull in terms of his teaching. English, a subject I later came to love, comprised mainly in his lessons of the instruction to turn to Burton Book 1 or 2 or Rideout Book 1, page whatever to page whatever, exercise whatever to exercise whatever and get on with them. If the lesson was in the afternoon Mr Heseltine would send one of the class, usually Micky Abrams, to the kitchen to fetch him a cup of tea and some biscuits. Probably not a teaching approach that would earn high marks with Ofsted today.

There were around twenty of us on the trip and they included two good friends, Colin Morris and Micky Abrams. Colin was a large lad, wryly humorous and even slightly eccentric. His father was a postman and he lived in Small Heath, then as now a solidly working class area of the city. However, like me, Colin had a country connection through some family friends in Worcestershire and developed a love of rural life. In particular, Colin rode horses. He did not of course own one but I seem to remember he helped out in a stable and got rides in return. This interest in horses and horse riding was pretty well unique among anyone I knew at the time and the subject of much comment by our group of friends. I think most of us saw it as profoundly weird and something we associated with snotty upper-class girls rather than working class city lads.

Micky Abrams was developing as a legend. He was bigger and much older looking than most of us. He was a teller of tall tales which many of us, myself included, were half inclined to believe. Or perhaps we just wanted to believe for example that a thirteen year old boy who was a friend of ours really had gone to London the weekend before and really had been seduced by a sexy 18 year old with whom he then spent a steamy couple of nights. Perhaps it made us feel that bit closer to the unattainable and scarcely imaginable world of sex and sophistication. I had only been once to London and that had been for my eighth or ninth birthday with my mum and Auntie Joan for a day trip by coach from Digbeth. So the idea of a weekend in London spent with some woman was as foreign and exciting to me as Venice. Micky was also a bold, not to say reckless, player-up of teachers. His playing up was however witty rather than vicious and at times almost surreal in what his imagination came up with. Mr Heseltine had some kind of connection with Micky's family either through the synagogue or the wider local Jewish community but this did not lead to Micky showing any greater respect or restraint in his lessons. Having drunk the tea that had been fetched for him, Mr Heseltine would then ask a boy to take it back. Again this was often Micky. On one occasion he made this request and Micky simply said no. Mr Heseltine clearly not believing him said;

– Here, catch.

And made as if to toss the cup to Micky.

– I won't catch it, so I wouldn't throw it.

Mr Heseltine seeing this as mere bravado lobbed the cup gently towards him. Micky stepped aside and the cup smashed on the floor.

– I said not to throw it.

The trip took place in the summer term. I was given some spending money, I think it was £5 and we met the coach with the rest of the party early in the morning on Broad Street by the Memorial Hall. We were to travel down to Waterloo by coach then train to Folkstone, boat across, and train from Boulogne to Venice. I was also given some sandwiches to eat packed in a tin. Such was my excitement that I forgot all about these. This was to have consequences days later.

The idea of being in a foreign country was for me a remarkable concept. As the cross-channel ferry approached the dock and as we prepared to disembark the excitement and anticipation built within me. There, a matter of feet from where I was standing was France, an entirely different, entirely foreign place. As I walked down the gang-plank towards the dock-side the excitement focused on which foot would be the first to touch foreign soil. It was my left foot.

I had a number of pre-conceptions in my head about being abroad. The first was that it would be hot. Even though we had crossed little more than twenty miles of sea my expectation was that I would be met by a dazzling sun and fierce heat. It was in fact late afternoon and needless to say the weather in Boulogne exactly mirrored that in Folkstone.

However, I was not disappointed in other ways. France, even only twenty miles to the south was entirely other, entirely different. The trains were higher and you went up a series of steps to them. The houses as we pulled out of the station were distinctly French, the electric pylons and telephone poles were unfamiliar in shape, the lay-out of the fields as we passed through the countryside was utterly distinct from those of England with a general absence of hedges. As the night advanced and we passed through the towns and cities of north-eastern and then eastern France each station seemed miraculously distinct, and the sound of announcements in a foreign language was compelling.

We sat up most of the night and had little sleep but eventually we did drift off after being told several times by Mr Heseltine to keep the noise down. When we awoke it was to the wondrous sight of the Alps. The train moved in and out of tunnels. The track ran alongside steep ravines with fast flowing streams at their base. At other times it skirted the sides of looming mountains. From time to time a great snow capped peak would lift itself above the lower mountains. It was a breathtaking experience.

We crossed the great flat plain of Lombardy, through Milan and on towards Venice. Towards the middle of the afternoon we approached the coast and the bridge that would take us across the lagoon to Venice. This was a grim and dispiriting sight. The coast at this point is full of sprawling industrial and petro-chemical sites, the bridge is flanked by line after line of electric pylons. It was profoundly depressing and our spirits fell as we contemplated spending a week in a landscape that made even the worst of the West Midland's conurbation look attractive.

The train entered Santa Lucia station and much chastened, tired and demoralised I stepped off. We gathered together and the party met with a guide who was awaiting us and who would take us on to our hotel. We walked down the platform and out of the station.

What an extraordinary, miraculous transformation! You come into the station directly from the bridge and the nightmarish industrial landscape. You exit onto a view of the Grand Canal that could have been painted by Canaletto. The steps in front of the station sloped down to the water's edge and the bustle of vaporetti, sleek polished wood covered taxi boats and gondolas. The water glittering in the brilliant afternoon sun. The sweep of the Grand Canal lined by the great palaces, the sloping striped mooring poles and the elegantly humped bridges crossing the smaller canals, the blue sky and the heat; all in that first and never to be erased image of Venice.

We stepped into a vaporetto and were whisked off to our hotel, a few minutes away and only a block or so from the Grand Canal itself. It was a modest hotel but spotlessly clean. We shared bedrooms with four or six to a room. The staff spoke little or no English and we of course spoke no Italian, but somehow or other we communicated as much as we needed and got by.

I cannot be sure whether or not this was the first time abroad for all of the group, but certainly it was for all of the ones I spent time with. The trip was full board with breakfast, packed lunch and an evening meal. We were at our most parochial and obnoxious at meal times. Along with most other English people I knew at the time, we had the view, unsullied by any evidence whatsoever, that foreign food was "oily" or "greasy". This mind you from a people who generally fried in lard. Olive oil in Birmingham was sold in chemists in tiny bottles and was used to clear wax from the ear. The idea of cooking in it, or worse still, coating salad in it, was revolting. There we were therefore, being served what was probably some of the most authentic Italian food, and turning our noses up at it and making derogatory noises and comments about it. The few who genuinely seemed to like it were labelled as hogs who would eat any swill. It would have been inconceivable to the twelve year old boy I then was that as an adult Italian food would become my favourite cuisine. Thus we went hungry in the evenings and filled ourselves up on the packed lunches, fruit from market stalls, cakes and chocolates. Towards the end of the week the cooking staff must have admitted defeat and began to serve us helpings of chips with most meals. God knows what they made of us as we rejected the pasta courses and the bulk of the main courses, stared with disgust at the dressed green salads but descended with relish on the french fries.

The visit was a mixture of organised activities and free time. The activities included a gondola ride, visits to the market, the Lido, the glassworks of Murano and the Doge's Palace. The latter was with a guide. It was a very hot day and the succession of grand rooms and massive paintings seemed endless. We were parched and tired and bored. We began to repeat aloud the refrain of the guide which appeared to introduce each new picture or artefact;

– When Venice was the richest and most powerful republic on earth...

Our respect for culture and history was not evident in our responses it has to be said. We longed to be out and drinking ice cold coca-cola at one of the cafes, a drink that was a new and exciting discovery for most of us and which certainly ranked above yet another Veronese or Tintoretto in our estimations.

The gondola ride took us along the Grand Canal and around some of the smaller back canals. Our main interest as I remember seemed to be encouraging the gondolier to race and overtake the others in our party. The markets were exciting and we followed up the guided visit with our own informal trips. My mother sent me an additional ten shilling note for spending money in a letter and I was able to change it at a stall. The currency was a wonder to us. At 1750 lira to the pound we marvelled at labels on items like washing machines that ran into the hundreds of thousands of lira. We bought trinkets from the stalls as well as fruit and slices of coconut that had been kept cool under tiny fountains. We were particularly fascinated by the shops that sold flick knives and discussed endlessly whether or not we would be able to get one past the teacher and then past customs. I managed to get a leather key ring holder and a wallet from one stall as presents for my father. Murano and the glass factory kept our attention until the heat drained it from us and the local shops provided me with several more presents for relatives. The boat trip out was a highlight as we passed a funeral gondola slowly rowing out a flower covered coffin to the cemetery island of San Michele. The most popular organised event, not surprisingly perhaps, was the visit to the Lido with its beaches where we could swim and lounge on sunbeds in the summer sun.

But what I remember most often and most warmly was the casual and unplanned wandering around the city with Micky and Colin. Often we were lost as we tried to negotiate the endless small squares, the calle and the winding routes along and across small canals. We would recognise a landmark only to get lost again and end up in the same place. In this way we became more familiar over the week with the city away from San Marco Square and the famous landmarks. As we wandered, purposefully or lost, we came across sudden and wonderful views of the lagoon or the Grand Canal, of Giudecca or San Giorgio Maggiore. More than this for me was the simple pleasure of the astonishing difference of this place in all its detail, in all its mundane everyday life, so different from the life and city I lived in. And the intense contrast of light, a light so much brighter than home, reflecting from the sparkling waters, contrasting sharply with the dark as you moved into the shadows of an alley or secluded piazza. Some evenings after our meal the three of us would wander up past San Marco and out along the Riva degli Schiavoni towards the Bienale where we would sit looking out across the Canale di San Marco, perhaps hoping for the much longed for but entirely unrealised meeting with some Italian girls but contented despite this disappointment to sit in the warm evening air in that magical place.

At some point mid-week I remembered my packed lunch from home. It was still in my holdall. I knew that it would be inedible and probably mouldy but I was not prepared for what I found on opening it, a mass of crawling maggots. I was revolted by the sight and lacked the determination to do what any sensible person would have done, empty the tin in a bin outside and wash it out. Instead, alone as I was and unobserved I simply dropped the tin in the bedroom litter bin. Needless to say the cleaning staff were not best pleased and complained to Mr Heseltine. I am afraid I did not own up.

As a group our behaviour was not always of the best. Mr Heseltine, who was known throughout the school as Sid, was obviously receiving a number of complaints from hotel staff and from our guides. His first line of sanction was to put a stop on our spending money which had been given to him by parents for safekeeping. A popular song at the time was *Right Said Fred* by Bernard Cribbins about a series of more and more destructive and comic actions by a group of inept removal men trying to shift a piano. We adapted the song;

   – "Right said Sid, have to stop the money, that there money's going to have to go.

   Were we in trouble..."

The monetary blockade clearly did not have the desired effect so there was a need for escalation. Sid informed us that such was the level of disgust at our behaviour that we were to be evicted from the hotel and must pack immediately to prepare for early departure home. It did not occur to us at the time that tickets would have been booked for a specific train and ferry and a coach booked at a set time and date from London. As we gathered with our luggage on the steps of the hotel overlooking a small canal, we were sufficiently cowed by the threat of imminent eviction to promise a genuine improvement. Sid played this cleverly. He was not at all sure the management of the hotel would take us back, not at all sure, but he would make the probably forlorn effort to plead on our behalf. He then disappeared back inside the hotel. We waited thoroughly convinced of a disgraceful early return to Brum. At last Sid returned. Well, they had not been at all keen at first and had refused to change their mind. He, however, had persevered and given them his solemn word that we would be much improved in our attitude and behaviour. At last after much persuasion they had reluctantly given way but with the clear message that any further infringement of the rules on our part would lead to instant eviction. We believed it all. Or perhaps I should say, I believed it all and was much shocked to hear one of the more cynical of our party suggest it was;

– A load of bollocks!

Whatever the case was in reality, the strategy worked in that there were no more complaints about us, no more financial sanctions and no more dire threats of an early return home.

On the last evening in Venice there was an event on the Grand Canal. I have no idea now exactly what this event was, it certainly was not the right time of the year for the carnival. Whatever this event was, or whatever it was to commemorate or celebrate, it was spectacular. We gathered on the steps down to the Grand Canal around the corner from the hotel. As darkness fell brightly lit boats and gondolas went past and from some of them there was the sound of arias from operas or popular Italian songs. With the sound, the warm evening, the great buildings along the canal and the lights reflecting on the water it was an extraordinary experience that I remember now only in the most impressionistic of fashions, but that impression runs deep.

It may have been true that I failed to appreciate the cultural highlights of Venice, that I favoured coca-cola over the glories of the Venetian renaissance, but Venice imprinted on my memory a profound image that has endured for over fifty years. It was my first visit abroad and it possesses therefore a special place in my memory that no subsequent foreign trip has or ever will equal. I have visited Venice many times since and never once did it disappoint me. This first visit planted a profound affection, not only for Venice, but for Italy, which remains my favourite foreign country.

I owe a great debt of gratitude to my parents for this visit, for the memories it created and the love of a most extraordinary city that it founded. I am grateful perhaps even more for the kindness they showed in making what must have been a considerable financial sacrifice in order to give me an opportunity and experience they had not had themselves. It was a small but deeply significant example of an aspiration on their part that my life would be richer than theirs, an example of parental affection and altruism. I hope that I at least attempted to make clear to them at some stage my deep appreciation.

15

Two Deaths

TO A YOUNG child death often seems remote both in terms of time and direct experience. When he or she comes into direct contact with it therefore there is little to draw on for defence. There were in my childhood a number of older relatives who died but no one close and therefore the impact of these losses was slight. There were however two occasions when the impact was direct and shocking.

I am ten years old. I am in the final year of primary school, I have a good circle of friends, a range of sports and interests and life jogs along pretty comfortably. It's a sunny morning and I arrive in school to meet friends so that we can play before registration time or chat about what we did the night before. As I enter the playground I am immediately aware of a difference. Children are not playing. They are gathered in small huddles and all seem to be involved in deep discussion.

As I cross the rear playground a lad I know meets me with the news that there has been a road accident and a boy from the school has been killed. He names him. He is not in my class and is not a boy I know well at all. My response is the mild kind of sadness we feel when we hear of the death of someone we know only vaguely or not at all.

I walk on to join my friends under the trees at the end of the main playground. Their expressions are serious and they look at me with concern. Had they heard, I ask, of the accident and I name the boy.

– No it's not him. It's Robert Rowley.

Though from a year below me, Robert was a good friend. Along with Paul Mallinder and me he was a member of the Frankley Beeches cub scouts. He lived in a road near to me and some days we walked into school together. They had got it wrong. It could not be Robert. Robert was a friend.

I protested that they were mistaken. I had been told who it was and I named the lad. I waited for them to check and admit their error. There was, however, no such error. Everyone I spoke to confirmed that it was indeed Robert. Crossing the Bristol Road South he had been hit by a car travelling at speed. The impact had flung him high into the air and back onto the road.

It was the first time in my life that death had taken someone who was close. Someone who was a daily part of my life. Someone engaged in the activities that I engaged in. Someone for whom I had the affection of friendship. It was also the first clear and direct indication that death was not reserved for the old; for people who had lived what to me were an unimaginable number of years; people for whom death was an ever expected outcome. Here was a clear intimation, the first intimation, of the randomness of death, "that we know not the hour of its coming".

As we talked I began to weep. Paul urged me not to cry with the wonderfully old fashioned line that while they as a group of friends understood, the girls would not and it would look bad for me. I think looking back that even at 10 years of age Paul would have made one of those wonderfully stoical First World War officers or Battle of Britain pilots who talk with such restrained sadness about the loss of friends. I am not a stoic. Was not then and never have been.

I have no recall what happened during the school day. This was not an age of counselling. Whether or not there was a special assembly I cannot remember. On my return home I found that mum had already heard of the accident. We had our meal. I did not play out and it was time for bed. Now for the first time I was alone with my thoughts about this tragedy.

I would never see Robert again. The finality of death was absolute. He had been here the day before. He had been a presence I had confidently expected to move forward with me through childhood and youth. He had had an undoubted future. What that future might be was of course, unknown, but it was a future. The choices of life were all before him. All to be made. Now for Robert there was no future. He was gone. The choices and uncertainties would remain forever unknown. For me and for all who had known him he would be forever a nine year old boy. This sense of death's ruthless finality was the first feeling that struck me. It was a sense of the full loss of a friend. But then another more selfish but far more powerful, far more horrifying fear grew. Robert's annihilation, the total disappearance of a unique person, a distinct consciousness who was as real as me announced that at some point the same fate awaited me. I too would be nothing. The fear and panic this evoked was almost overwhelming. I was sobbing uncontrollably. Mum, seated on the end of my bed, tried to comfort me.

– I don't want to die, I sobbed.

I saw in that moment the look of pure anguish on her part. It was the anguish of knowing that this was not a fear she could assuage. The inevitability of death cannot be driven away even by the most loving of parents. I saw this and recognised it with a terrible certainty. It was a moment of first division from the certainties and securities of childhood. I had been confident in my parents' ability to protect me. Here was a challenge they could not meet, my fear of death.

Once again it is summer. This time early evening not morning. I am fourteen years old and I am in the front room doing my homework in a desultory sort of way. There is a ring on the front door bell. Dad goes to the door. It's Les Baldwin. There has been an accident. His eldest daughter Lesley has been knocked over crossing Frankley Beeches Road. Would my dad go with him to the hospital. Dad leaves immediately to drive Mr Baldwin to the hospital.

The Baldwins lived across the road from me at 27 Fairway. Les, was from the Welsh valleys and like his neighbour Mr Taylor had settled in Birmingham to work at Longbridge. Mrs Baldwin was from Lancashire. They had three children. The youngest Lloyd was one of the most mischievous but good natured of small boys. Despite his naughtiness he was very much liked as a kind of Dennis the Menace figure. Beverley, the younger of two girls, I did not know well as she was several years my junior. Lesley, the oldest, named after her father and almost certainly his favourite, though a year or two younger than me, was a close friend. As small children we had played as part of a group together in the street. Later as teenagers we spent time talking, though we had our separate lives and groups of friends away from Fairway.

Mum goes across the road to be with Mrs Baldwin and her mother-in-law. And to wait. I am not alarmed. I have little doubt that Lesley will be fine. There will be some injuries but she will be back to be cried over and chastised for failing to take care crossing the road.

I see the car pull up opposite. Mum comes out to meet dad. I see him shake his head. And I know.

Lesley's injuries had been dreadful and she had died on or soon after arrival at hospital.

This time the impact was different. Yes, there was the loss of a dear friend, someone I had known for many years, someone I had seen grow from a little girl into a young teenager. Yes, again it was a reminder of the imminence of death and of its random nature. But what was different this time was seeing so closely, so terribly its brutal impact on the parents.

Lesley had been their first born child. They did not I am sure love her more than Lloyd or Beverly, but their hopes for her, their obvious pride in her, were so strong. She would now be an absence that would be ever present in their lives. Mrs Baldwin must have felt the loss as strongly and deeply as her husband. But somehow or other she carried on. Mr Baldwin, however, was changed forever. All joy seemed to go from him. His deep grief and sadness were palpable.

Tragedy is rarely even-handed. You would hope that the loss of Lesley would represent the share of terrible grief doled out to one family. Years later, a successful and aspiring nurse in her twenties, their surviving daughter Beverly collapsed and died from a massive brain haemorrhage. I had left Birmingham by this time and my family had moved from Fairway but Mrs Baldwin and my mother maintained contact. Mr Baldwin died soon after. Like the incident in the graveyard at East Woodlands the story of the Baldwin family was an example in real life of the accumulation of terrible blows that seem implausibly unremitting in a novelist like Hardy but which do sometimes occur to real and ordinary people.

tended to lay emphasis on the Gospel message about the duty of care to the poor, the weak and the excluded. These were men and women who were, in a very genuine sense, good, and who felt passionately that they had a mission to act in the interests of and alongside those less fortunate than themselves. They did not preach at us. What was impressive looking back, was the extent to which they avoided trying simply to convince or persuade us and the degree to which they tried to open our minds and encourage us to think for ourselves. What they insisted on was not that we should agree, but that we should take an interest and that having taken an interest and adopted a view, a moral stance, that we should act upon it.

I need to be honest here. Moral enlightenment was not my only and almost certainly not my prime motive for attending the YPF. Several friends went and a number of very attractive girls. There was a mid-week youth club with the usual range of games and the usual range of social opportunities to get to know some of the rather sexier young Methodists, a combination of adjective and noun that may not naturally spring to mind. Nevertheless, though my motives may have been venal, even carnal, the lasting impact was moral and political.

Paul, one of the YPF leaders was a very earnest young man with a strong Christian faith and a deep commitment to some of the key moral and political struggles of the day. One Sunday morning he ran a film for us. It was a grainy black and white 16mm film projected onto one of the light coloured walls of the meeting room. Near the beginning a child is hit by a car and critically injured. His life is clearly in the balance and time is of the essence in terms of getting hospital treatment. An ambulance and medical crew arrive. However, as they move to give treatment to the child they are prevented from doing so by those gathered nearby. The ambulance and crew are forced to leave. A second ambulance arrives but the child is by this time past help and dies. The child was white. The first ambulance had a black team and was designated for the use of black and coloured patients only. This was apartheid South Africa in the 1960s.

What I think first struck us was the madness of it with the implied logic that it was better for a child to die than to be treated by people of the "wrong" colour. Insane. What followed was input from a guest speaker about what the apartheid regime stood for, examples of its crazy laws and the vicious and evil treatment that it handed out to the majority of the population in the interests of white supremacy. The story now is well known and the fall of the apartheid state an established historical event. In the mid-1960s there were of course those heroic figures in South Africa and in the UK who valiantly opposed apartheid and racism in general. However, it did not have the mass and popular base it later achieved. Those who spoke out against apartheid in South Africa or racism in Britain were a relatively small group. Openly racist behaviour and discrimination was still legal in Britain at the time. Racist terms of abuse were openly used and rarely if ever challenged. So it is little surprise that what shocked us at first was the perverted logic of the event we had been shown and not the moral abomination it was based upon.

Gradually the speaker and Paul led us into a discussion that provoked thought about the moral issues related to any system in which people might be discriminated against on the grounds of their colour, their ethnic origins or their religious convictions. It is unlikely that any of the young people in the room that morning were hardened racist bigots. It is, however, very likely that most or all of us shared many of the casual assumptions about ethnic and cultural differences that were common at that time. Paul and the speaker had a deep-rooted moral objection, even a visceral disgust at apartheid that was based on a view that all humans were divinely created and all were equally deserving of respect and dignity. They were convinced that racism in general, and apartheid in particular, were anathema to the fundamental message of the Gospels.

It is unlikely that this event by itself dispelled my inherent racial or cultural prejudices, prejudices that I almost certainly failed even to acknowledge. What it did was to open a process of moral and logical questioning about a profound and complex issue. It was also, and equally important, a powerful example of the way in which some adults stood by a code of religious and moral convictions that informed their view of controversial issues as well as shaping their daily conduct.

We were addressed on another occasion by a trade union official. He outlined for us the history of trade unionism and the basic role of a union to protect its members and promote their interests through collective representation and action. Now for me unions had only ever been talked about as a negative force. Unions were the obstruction to progress as far as my father was concerned. His view was that it was up to each worker to negotiate his or her terms with the managers. It was ironic that years later when the firm he worked for sold out, as a non-union member he was left with little or no protection and, after many years of hard-work and good service, he was simply made redundant. Here at the YPF was someone arguing that unions had been a force for good. They had, he argued, been responsible for improvements in working conditions and had given the relatively powerless a voice and influence. Again, this was not a moment of conversion on the road to Damascus, but it was at the very least the planting of a doubt. The doubt led first to a questioning of an unquestioned distrust of unions and later to a committed belief in their value. That position was arrived at eventually years later but the YPF session cleared at least some space in my mind for debate, for persuasion.

An event that excited a great deal of controversy in the late 60s and early 70s was the Vietnam War. It was an issue for a smaller number of activists in the mid-60s. YPF debated this issue. We were faced with proponents on both side of the argument, persuasive people of integrity who held conflicting views. We were also shown documentaries that explored the matter further. This time it was a Pauline conversion as far as I was concerned. It was dramatic and almost instant. From being scarcely aware that the war was happening I rapidly became an ardent opponent of US involvement in Vietnam. I attended meetings, spoke and even wrote a short, very emotive piece on the subject that was published in the Methodist Newsletter. Much of what I said or wrote was raw, immature and historically poorly informed. But it was strongly felt and the indignation was at the very least a human response to what I saw as injustice and barbarity.

My final and abiding memory of the YPF was one evening in November of 1965 following a youth club meeting seeing one of the senior members of the church, a man probably in his fifties or sixties, in obvious distress. We asked Paul about this. Deeply moved himself, Paul told us the man had been a lifelong pacifist and was deeply attached to that belief. However, he regarded the white Rhodesian government's declaration of unilateral independence that month as an act so heinous and so likely to lead to racial oppression that he found himself seriously contemplating a position advocating the use of armed intervention to overthrow the Smith regime. Such was the shock to his core values of this contemplation that he was thrown into a state of moral perturbation and open distress. I had never seen an adult respond in such a way to an external world event that did not touch him directly.

My brief flirtation with Christian commitment faded by the time I was about 17. I have not returned to it since. What stayed with me was the inspiration of people who thought deeply and honestly about major moral and political issues; people who were motivated not by self or group interest but a sense of right and wrong, by a deep conviction that where we stand on matters of justice and compassion matters. Further, that these issues are not for moral contemplation alone but for action. I have not always lived up to these values by a long way but they have been important to me and have provided a framework of reference that remains relevant.

17

This Old Heart of Mine

MINE WAS not a musical family. Dad had a pleasant tenor voice but rarely sang. Mum had been told in school not to sing along with the class as she was what the teacher described as "a growler". She did indeed find it difficult to locate or hold a tune but often, usually when she thought she would not be over-heard, she would sing softly, out of key, to herself. The two songs I recall her singing were, *Red Sails in the Sunset* and *(I'll be with you) In Apple Blossom Time*. The first was written in 1935 and the second in 1920 but significantly both were later recorded by Nat King Cole, a singer much admired by my parents. I suppose therefore these two songs constitute my earliest and perhaps most poignant musical memories. I sometimes wonder, sadly, what connotations the words of *In Apple Blossom Time* had for mum as her husband's love faded and her marriage began to fall apart;

"Happy the bride the sun shines on today!"

The 1950s was a period of great change in popular music. It was the decade in which Rock and Roll became the dominant popular music of a new generation of teenagers. It was a period in which the influence of American popular culture assumed its hegemony over first the western world and then the rest of the globe. I was aware of none of this. For me pop music in a form broadly recognisable to this day, sprang fully formed into my consciousness some time around the age of 11 or 12. My first record, a single, was bought for me at Christmas 1962. It was the hit song, *Bobby's Girl* by Susan

Maughan. It was fitting perhaps that my first record was by a star raised in Birmingham, not that I was aware of this at the time and not that it would have made any difference to me. Susan Maughan had a number of hits but this was the biggest. She had a powerful voice not dissimilar to Helen Shapiro and in the mould of Dusty Springfield though not quite as classy as that great singer. The song itself was lively and, what could best be termed, catchy. The lyrics would not recommend themselves to those wishing to raise the aspirations of young women today;

> "There's just one thing that I want to be
> I want to be Bobby's girl…"

I played this record, after all it was the sum total of my collection, over and over again, probably to the unspoken irritation of my parents.

Not long after came the Liverpool Sound. If you visit Liverpool now the focus is almost exclusively on The Beatles. There is a Beatles museum, Beatles tours, Beatles memorabilia and buskers on the streets singing Beatles songs. This is entirely understandable given what we now know about how this group developed and the grip it took on the world of pop music and pop culture. In 1963 this dominance was not yet so clear and the Liverpool Sound included a number of other very successful chart topping groups including, Billy J Kramer and the Dakotas, Gerry and the Pacemakers and The Searchers. In the summer of 63 we were on holiday in Devon and we spent one night in a Bed and Breakfast. The owner, very keen to show me that she was, what my mum always termed as "with it" in other words in tune with the latest fashion, said that she supposed I liked The Beatles best. No, I replied, I liked The Searchers and their song *Sweets for My Sweet*. Even then it seemed to me, in some obscure way, important to choose something not too obvious, though *Sweets for My Sweet* was hardly a deeply radical taste statement on my part given that it was at number one in the charts. I continued for a year or so to like British pop, and particularly the Mersey groups and songs like *How Do You Do It* by Gerry and the Pacemakers and *Bad to Me* by Billy J Kramer and the Dakotas. This was also the period in which I came across The Hollies.

Buying records was dependent on pocket money and therefore could be afforded only every few weeks. The collection founded on *Bobby's Girl* grew slowly and with no real guiding purpose beyond what took my fancy at the time. The radio was the main source of access to pop music. Modern listeners will find it hard to recognise the radio scene of the late 50s and early 60s. BBC had an effective monopoly although foreign stations could be picked up on many radios. The Light Programme offered the largest output of pop music though even this was very limited and was further restricted by the tight censorship exercised at the time. The Animals, a brilliant Newcastle group fronted by Eric Burdon, had a major hit with an old folk and Blues song, *The House of the Rising Sun* in 1964. There are many versions of this song. In many the subject of the song is a woman degraded by her gambler lover and with the strong suggestion that she is now a prostitute in the brothel, *The House of the Rising Sun*;

> "O mothers go tell your children,
> Not to do what I have done,
> To spend your life in sin and misery,
> In the House of the Rising Sun."

Perhaps to avoid some of the controversy, The Animals sang from the point of view of a man who is degraded by drink and gambling. It's a great and powerful song and The Animals' performance is potent. It rose to number one in the charts. The BBC was wracked with indecision about whether a song that had associations with a brothel in other versions could be played on the airwaves.

In 1967 the Stones produced a double-sided hit, *Let's Spend the Night Together* and *Ruby Tuesday*. Again the BBC engaged in moral agonising about whether it was appropriate to play a song that appeared to celebrate sex outside marriage. The Stones produced a counter argument that the song could simply be seen as a request to spend time together, after all, they said, young people sometimes spent all night at parties. Listen to the lyrics and see if you are convinced by this argument. I love the idea that this song can be presented as simply wanting to spend a night together innocently at some party, I suppose the satisfaction of "every need" would consist of fetching her a soft drink whenever she was thirsty or some crisps when she hungered. The fact that such a defence had to be made, and made with the usual Jagger tongue-in-cheek style, tells us much about the difference between the moral climate then and now. The BBC adopted the stance of moral arbiter. It saw itself as protecting the morality of the nation. More specifically its position was one that suggested that the working classes, and the young working classes in particular, needed to be protected from the corrupting influence of pop music and pop culture. This was a period of ardent debate about the corrupting influence of the media and of TV in particular with earnest debates involving such figures as Malcolm Muggeridge and populist moral crusades led by people like Mary Whitehouse. Needless to say such campaigns tended to increase rather than decrease the sale of such records.

I have said that it was possible to pick up foreign stations and it is hard to give an impression of just how liberating one of these was for me in my teens. The station was Radio Luxembourg with its programmes of uninterrupted and, as far as I was aware, uncensored pop music. Reception was intermittent with programmes fading in and out but I would take a transistor radio into the front room where I was supposed to be concentrating on my homework and listen to it for hours. Radio Luxembourg was a commercial station and the sworn enemy of the BBC and all it stood for. It was in many ways a precursor of the pirate stations, like Caroline, that have attracted more glamorous attention in recent years. Its programmes were funded by adverts. The most memorable, and one that can be quoted practically verbatim by Luxembourg listeners of my generation, was the Horace Batchelor Infradraw method. This may sound like an obscure means of Catholic contraception but in fact was an advertisement for what was presented as a highly successful means of predicting the results for the football pools. It was clearly produced on the cheap with Horace himself in his marked West Country accent urging us to contact him via his address in;

"Keynsham, that's K-E-Y-N-S-H-A-M, Keynsham, Bristol..."

Up to about 1964 my taste was pretty middle of the road pop. At that point there was the emergence of the mods and their smarter, slightly later offshoot, the townies with their two piece, mohair suits and the music that was to dominate my interest in pop from then on, Tamla and soul. My mentor and taste adviser, in clothes, hair and music, was my friend Mark. He was well ahead of me in term of social life and musical knowledge. Tamla was of course the successful cross-cultural embodiment of black American music pioneered by Gordie and others in Detroit. Tamla seemed to have access to an inexhaustible supply of gifted solo singers and groups both male and female. Early groups like The Contours and singers like Eddie Holland gave way to hugely successful performers like, Jimmy Ruffin, Marvin Gaye, The Supremes, Martha Reeves and the Vandellas, the Jackson Five, Stevie Wonder, Gladys Knight and the Pips and The Four Tops. My personal favourites at the time were, however, The Temptations led in the first instance by the talented but flawed David Ruffin. My first ever pop LP, bought with money earned from working in my dad's shop was *Temptations with a Lot of Soul*. However, if they were my favourite group, the absolute pinnacle of Tamla for many of us in my circle was the great Isley Brothers' song, *This Old Heart of Mine*. As I grew older and began to go out, Mark and others directed me towards the kind of places that played Tamla and soul. Principal among these was the Rainbow Suite on New Street. This club was above the Co-op Store and was accessed via a lift. There were live groups but my dominant memory of the Rainbow is of records being played, and all of them pretty well being black American, Tamla, Stax or Atlantic label based. There was a bar off the corridor somewhere and the fashionable drink for me and my friends was bitter and lime, a pint of bitter with a dash of lime juice. For the girls I seem to remember it was Black Velvet, rum with a dash of blackcurrant. These drinks are a reminder that not everything retro is cool.

Stax and Atlantic, two labels that later merged, were the source of a more serious, in many ways higher quality and classier form of pop than Tamla. On these labels were the great black American soul singers often coming out of a Gospel singing background as was the case with Aretha Franklin. Other favourites included, Wilson Pickett, Sam and Dave and Carla Thomas. However, perhaps in part because of his early death, it was Otis Redding who attained the most legendary status of them all.

Access to the best of black American music was greatly enhanced by the wonderful Diskery. This store, still going strong just off Bristol Street, had an astounding collection of LPs, many straight from the US and not available elsewhere. Buying records from Stax, Atlantic or Tamla that were not on sale in mainstream UK record shops seemed a point almost of honour at the time.

As I have said, ours was not a musical family. No one played an instrument. There was no thought of music lessons. My access to the music that later came to dominate, though never exclusively, my musical taste, was by chance. I had heard and had in fact been bought the *1812 Overture* by Tchaikovsky, but though I enjoyed it, it did not spark any wider interest in classical music. Dad worked in a shop that sold radiograms and record players. They would use records to demonstrate the products to potential customers. They would offer a range of types of music, including a small sample of classical LPs. When these records became too scratched or warped to serve their purpose they were discarded. From time to time dad would bring home one of these records. Alone in the house and out of curiosity I took one of these discarded albums from its cover and put it on the record player. Being ignorant of the piece I put the second side on first by mistake. It was one of the most fortunate cultural mistakes of my life. What I heard was a heart-breakingly poignant and beautiful introduction by the orchestra followed by the chords of the piano, slowly picking up the theme. Its impact was dramatic. For the first time I was deeply moved, almost to tears by the beauty of a sound. Nothing before had ever provoked such a feeling of both beauty and profound emotional depth. It was the second movement of Beethoven's 5th Piano Concerto, *The Emperor*. By such odd chances, a scratched and discarded record put on second side first in this case, are our lives sometimes enriched beyond expectation. Such was the case here and this time it did open, though tentatively at first, the world of classical music. It is a piece I still cherish.

I was never a real mod or towney like Mark, his brother and their friends from Quinton. I was never really cool enough or smartly dressed enough at the time but I loved the music then and still do. A few years ago I attended Mark and his wife Gill's 60th birthday celebrations. We were talking about old times when a record came on. Mark and Gill immediately rose;

– Sorry, we have to dance to this.

It was *This Old Heart of Mine*. And they still moved better than I ever did.

18

And so to school:
Part 3 – The Sixth Form

I WAS ON holiday on the Isle of Wight in the August of 1966 when my 'O' Level results came out. My Auntie Rhona had agreed to pick them up for me so it was with considerable anxiety that I rang her from a phone box in Cowes.

– You've done really well, she assured me.

But when I listened to the list of grades it was very clear that there was a huge divide between English, Geography, RE and History where I had got top grades, and maths where I had scraped through and Biology, Physics, Chemistry and French where I had done badly.

I blame the warm weather of that summer. It was too great a temptation to sit out in the garden during revision leave. Surely I could revise just as well out there? Well, the answer to that was no I could not. The books and papers got in the way of the sunbathing and dozing off was a constant distraction from serious study. Besides which my revision method was shaky at best comprising as it did the endless reading and re-reading of my notes. What was vague or confusing at first became more vague and more confusing with each re-reading. The stubborn belief that some of it would stick by the process of mechanically turning the pages and lightly applying the sight was not effective. It did not stick. The experience of the exams strongly suggested as much and the results provided quantifiable evidence. Consequently the subjects that I did well in were those where I already had a genuine interest and very sound grasp of the material. The subjects where I needed to revise were the ones that suffered from this approach.

Anyway come September I would be returning to school as part of the sixth form. When I had arrived at the school five years earlier sixth formers had appeared like men to me, especially the few who already had fully formed five o'clock shadows and sideburns. Now I was a sixth former, albeit with neither a five o'clock shadow or sideburns. The regime for sixth formers was still strict by modern standards but relaxed by that of the lower school. We had privileges. We wore a different tie. We could enter the school by the main front doors. We could use the glass sided corridor that linked the science, woodwork and arts block to the rest of the school. We could study in the library in our "free periods". It may not sound much now but it seemed a lot and it seemed significant back then.

At 'A' Level I was studying history, English, scripture knowledge and general studies. The bad news was that Mr Champion, the inspirational teacher of RE, had left the school. He was replaced by Dr Pollock. Dr Pollock may have had many qualities and many skills, but teaching was not one of them. There were only two of us in the group, Duncan Skeen and me. Duncan was the only member of the sixth form to whom the word "cool", in the sense it might be applied to Miles Davies, could in any way be ascribed. Out of school his dress was unconventionally stylish. And what is more, he was seen, so we were reliably informed, coming out of the Cannon Hill Arts Centre with two incredibly beautiful black girls, one on each arm. He was also one of the very few who by the end of the lower sixth was genuinely and widely believed not to be a virgin. So it was me and Duncan and Dr Pollock.

The Doctor was reminiscent of one of those scholarly, dry characters in an M.R. James ghost story who get their comeuppance by being overly curious about some obscure text in a library. Whereas Mr Champion had encouraged a critical view of the Bible and its authorship and had indicated internal contradictions to be explored,

Dr Pollock was a committed evangelical and would brook no argument that might in any way question the Bible's divine inspiration and unshakeable accuracy and authority. This might make for good religion, at least in his terms, but it made for lousy scholarship and worse teaching. We were not steered to any of the critics who might have questioned such views. Eventually, Dr Pollock decided that the best way to teach us was simply to hand over his extensive, very extensive, notes, and let us copy them.

This style of teaching was not stimulating and perhaps as a consequence Duncan I developed techniques to unsettle him and to break the tedium of copying endless notes on the books of Kings and Prophets. We would engage him in theological debate. As his position remained steadfastly fixed and unshakeable so ours would become more and more extreme, not to say, heretical. Alternatively we quizzed him on moral issues.

- Sir, do you believe sex before marriage to be both against Scriptural guidance and Christian morality?
- Yes, indeed quite so. I believe Biblical guidance to be quite unambiguous and authoritative on this matter.
- Does this ban apply only to the act of sexual intercourse sir?
- By no means.
- Surely sir, all acts of physical affection might originate in and be expressions of sexual desire?
- Quite so. Hence the need for great restraint in such matters.
- And this could include could it not sir, kissing and embracing if motivated by sexual desire?
- Exactly so.
- But surely, even such gestures as hand-holding might be motivated by and may lead on to increased sexual desire and thus the temptation of more intense sexual activity, sir?

– It is for this very reason that I would advise that such gestures of physical attraction be reserved for partners who intend to marry.

The discussion ended at this point with neither Duncan or me fully convinced by this very clear and unequivocal moral guidance for our physical and spiritual welfare. Pollock baiting usually ended with some juicy piece of nonsense like this which could then be shared with others for their edification or amusement. It did on this occasion lead to an ongoing joke in which Duncan or I would seize the other's hand and then insist that we would now have to marry.

History was taught by two teachers, Mr Dykes, who had come fresh to the school a year or so before and Mr Butler. Mr Dykes was clearly a very able man and I thought a very good teacher in many ways. However, like many new teachers he struggled a bit with discipline and, though in the sixth form, we could be disruptive not to say down-right unpleasant at times. Still despite this I felt well taught by Mr Dykes and I liked him.

Mr Butler was a great teacher. His discipline was incredibly strong and lower down the school we had learned first by reputation and then by direct experience his prowess in the slippering department. He had been our form tutor in the third year and one day in Form Period he had ended up slippering almost the whole class when the queue to pay in the termly parental contribution to school funds and the queue to be slippered had got confused. Years later when I got to know him I asked how this had happened and was he not aware of the confusion? Yes, he said, but by the time he realised his mistake he was so far committed that he thought it best simply to carry on. Such was his aura of control that not one of the innocent thought to complain. As a history teacher he was wonderful. He was incredibly well informed and intellectually engaged. He was witty and his lessons were lively. While Mr Dykes was teaching us European history from 1453 to 1815, Mr Butler taught the other component, British History from 1714 to 1815. His approach was first to go through the period with us, setting out and testing with us the conventional political history with its tale of Whigs and Tories, Jacobite rebellions, unstable ministries, the wars with France, the Industrial Revolution, the loss of the American colonies and the Revolutionary and Napoleonic Wars. We had completed this with months to go.

We then looked at the century through the lens of a series of biographies, Walpole, Fielding, John Wilkes and so on. Finally, each of us chose one of a series of themes he offered and researched and presented it to the class. By the end of the course we had an understanding of the eighteenth century that was not only detailed but deep. It was a style of teaching that engaged interest and stimulated debate and thinking rather than simply preparing us for an exam. It was certainly more than good enough to maintain the interest and challenge the intellect of one of my classmates, David Cannadine, who went on to be a fine and eminent historian.

English Literature was taught by three teachers. One of them, whose name I have sadly forgotten was a well intentioned but ineffectual teacher who failed either to control the class or stimulate our interest in the two set books he taught, *Emma* by Jane Austen and the *Selected Poems* of Wordsworth. In one particularly dull lesson I watched fascinated while my friend Mark spent his time erasing the letter "e" from the title of the poem, "The Solitary Reaper". Sadly it was not until my mid twenties that a university lecturer kindled an interest in Wordsworth and not until I was nearly forty that I began to appreciate the subtle brilliance of Austen, such is the impact of poor teaching.

Mr Gadd taught Shakespeare and Chaucer. In our year the syllabus stipulated *Othello* and *Antony and Cleopatra* for the Shakespeare and the *General Prologue* and *Nun's Priest Tale* for the Chaucer. Frank, as he was known, kept iron control. He was a good teacher but he was inclined to savage sarcasm. We were expected to be able to support any comment, judgement or observation we made on the text with an accurate quotation from memory.

– Morris. Why does Enobarbus behave in this way?

– Because he feels guilty at deserting Antony, sir.

– Quote.

Silence.

– Now, you need to appreciate, examiners are simple creatures and they seem to like it if they feel you have read the text. So let's go back to the beginning, there is this man Shakespeare who wrote this play... got that Morris?

– Yes, sir.

Despite the constant anxiety about being the butt of his sarcasm we generally liked and respected him and I can still quote more from these two Shakespeare plays than from any of his other works.

The third English teacher was a remarkable man, Mr Hancocks, Dave as we familiarly called him, though not to his face. He had a violent temper which could explode at any felt slight or imagined impertinence. He was, however, a gifted and inspiring teacher. Like Mr Butler he took the view that the sixth form was a time for intellectual challenge and cultural awakening and not simply for the efficient mastery of the demands of an examination. He was teaching us the *Selected Poems* of T.S. Eliot and *A Portrait of the Artist as a Young Man* by James Joyce. If ever there were texts designed to appeal to a pretentious young man like me, these were the ones. They were difficult not to say obscure. They were radically different, more exciting than any other text I had read. Without any sense of self-irony or awareness of Joyce's irony, I identified completely with Stephen Dedalus the brilliant but arrogant and often unpleasant hero of the novel.

I had always been a reader but it had been in many ways quantity rather than quality. I had read few classic texts before going into the sixth form. I had read a massive number of detective novels and random other pieces. At the suggestion of Mr Hancocks I began a wider reading programme. It was water to a man crossing a desert. Ezra Pound through the connection with Eliot, Hardy, *Dubliners* by Joyce and then onto *Ulysses*, Dickens with *Great Expectations*,

Steinbeck and so on. It was a genuine awakening to just how much was available. My reading might have been naive. My self-image was undoubtedly inflated and misguided. My understanding might have been limited. But my enthusiasm was real and sustained a lifetime's habit of reading great literature. Then I may have thought I had read a lot. Now I feel more like Dedalus when he says to his mother that he has "read little and understood less."

General Studies was exactly what the label said: studies that were meant to offer a broader education. Teachers offered a range of short courses on a wide variety of subjects. For us this included a brief course on philosophy, as well as on-going lessons in Maths and French. It also included an introduction to Fortran. Computers at the time were still not accessible to schools. They cost millions of pounds and occupied whole suites of rooms. They were programmed by experts and any instructions to the computer had to be translated into one of the computer languages like Fortran or Cobalt. These instructions were then entered on punch cards. My grasp of this subject was pretty shaky at the time and even more so now. I do remember work on binary systems. I remember filling in sheets that were then sent off to be converted into punch cards and weeks later results coming back to class. My impression is that it required the equivalent of a PhD in Maths to actually instruct the computer which after several hours work produced the kind of calculation the average mobile phone would now manage in milliseconds with contemptuous ease.

Five Ways had prefects and sub-prefects. Under the leadership of the head boy and deputy head boy the prefects were expected to support discipline around the school. Before school prefects operated the late book, taking the names of any boys who were late and assigning them to the late detention that evening. At break and lunch time prefects were on duty around the corridors and outside the tuck-shop. Prefects and their supporting sub-prefects were expected to supervise a form group while it waited for the form tutor to come down to take the register after lunch. After school prefects were assigned to bus queues and were expected to police behaviour on any bus they were on. Prefects had powers. They could give essays out. They could also summon pupils to what were known as Prefects' Courts. This from my experience was an opportunity to humiliate boys by making them perform absurd tasks such as standing on one leg, rotating their arms and saying "I am a little red windmill." Typically, tougher boys were rarely summoned to the Court in this way.

The appointment of a new crop of prefects was quite a complex affair. A secretive activity a bit like the appointment of the Doge of Venice or the Pope. In the last half term of the Lower Sixth, the existing prefect body, under the guidance of a senior member of staff, appointed a group of pupils to be sub-prefects. A sub-prefect worked alongside the existing prefects and was assigned to one of them. Thus it was that I became a sub-prefect. I was almost certainly appointed on the urging of friends like Dickie Mapp and Rob Matthews who were in the school cross-country team with me and it was therefore no surprise that I was assigned to Dickie. On the last day of term a small group of the sub-prefects from the Lower Sixth were appointed full-prefects. To my considerable surprise I was named one of this group. It was our job to nominate the rest of the prefect body and to expand the cadre of sub-prefects.

Prefects had additional privileges. While sub-prefects wore only a badge to mark their office, we were expected to wear a blazer with white braid around the edges, a different tie and a badge. I remember my mother sewing on the braid with great pride. We also had a prefects' common room. This rather grand term conjures up the idea of an elegant room with leather chairs, green shaded lights, book-lined walls and a hushed atmosphere. This room did not really match this image of a common room. It was a small square room, probably designed as a stock-room. It was bare except for the few items of old furniture we scrounged. The walls were lined with pictures cut out from magazines. Added to the pictures were words coming out of the mouths of various royal, political and show-business celebrities that had been added over the months by us. Some of these comments were clever and witty, not a few were crass and downright disgusting and most were obscene. We thought they were very clever and clear evidence of our sophistication. The only luxury we had was a tape-recorder brought in by one of our number. On this was a selection of songs, mainly soul or Tamla Motown, or at least those are the ones I remember. Knocks on the door to ask for the "noise" to be turned down were a regular occurrence. Occasionally there would be a drive by staff to get prefects into the library during free periods. For a few weeks there would be a determined effort with daily notices to remind us that free periods were not in fact "free" but were "study periods" to be spent studying in the library. Checks would then be made on where we were during these periods and there would be raids on the common room to herd the disobedient along to the library. These activities were much resented by us. They were seen as an undisguised attempt to erode our privileges, undermine our dignity and status and bring us back into line. Fortunately for us the staff rarely had the energy to sustain the effort for long and things would then slip back into their old routine.

There was a Sixth Form Society which met at lunch times. How regular its meetings were I don't recall. In what was a period of cultural enthusiasm for me I offered to give a talk on the work of the post-Impressionist painter Gauguin. This was a suitably pretentious subject for me though I have to say in my own defence that such was my naivety that it never crossed my mind that it might be seen in this way. As far as I can remember it was quite well attended though God knows why. The whole of my expertise on this subject was based on one book about him and the fact that I had seen one of his paintings at the Barber Institute. However, what the talk lacked in real insight or technical knowledge, which by the way was considerable, it probably made up for in earnest enthusiasm and total confidence on the part of the speaker that this was cutting edge stuff.

In December 1967 the great soul singer Otis Redding was killed in a plane crash. Many of us were great fans of black American soul music and in particular we loved the music that was produced on the Stax-Atlantic label. Otis Redding was very high on our list of idols. His death, therefore, was significant to us. The Sixth Form Society was determined to mark this tragic event and a volunteer was found to make a tribute speech one lunchtime. It has to be said that he, nameless in my memory, was not one of those naturally gifted as a speaker but he had a very sympathetic audience. The talk was punctuated by tracks played from Otis Redding albums. However, as he went on even the most ardent fans of the great soul singer began to tire of the endlessly repeated line, interjected into virtually every sentence that Otis was;

– Surely the greatest soul singer of all time...

Late in his talk he introduced a track Otis Redding had recorded with Carla Thomas;

– Otis Redding and Carla Thomas...surely the greatest soul partnership of all time...

At this point a voice yelled out;

– What about Pearl Carr and Teddy Johnson – eh?

This somewhat broke the solemn mood. Pearl Carr and Teddy Johnson were not at the pinnacle of soul music. They were a husband and wife team who always looked as though they were dressed for a dinner party. They were regulars on light entertainment programmes in the 1950s and 60s and it is unlikely that they had any fans under the age of 40. They had represented the UK at the Eurovision Song Contest some years before with the distinctly un-soul like, "Sing Little Birdie." They had finished second.

It is easy to look back and laugh at the cultural and intellectual pretensions of my seventeen year old self. I certainly took myself very seriously at the time and made claims for myself as a man of culture that appear somewhat ridiculous now. What I can still, however, appreciate is just how exciting and transformative this period was for me. I did not come from a family that had a deep interest in culture. My mother read books, mainly Mills and Boon and my father read too, an eclectic mix of non-fiction, often focused around war and history. In later life my mother, through a colleague at work, developed an interest in poetry and novels including interestingly, T.S. Eliot. They had also taken the trouble on holidays to take me to castles and old churches, partly because they liked them and partly because they thought it would interest me. They were both highly intelligent people who had not had the educational opportunities I was to get, opportunities that opened up a sense of just how much was available culturally and that instilled enough confidence in me to begin to take advantage of this knowledge.

I have already mentioned the world of classic literature that was opened up to me by my teachers and how this encouraged an ambitious approach to reading that included not only literature itself but the beginnings of an interest in literary criticism and theory. What also happened was a sudden and, in some ways, inexplicable interest in other areas of the arts. In part I think I was spurred on by an image of what an "intellectual" ought to do and ought to be interested in. In part, there was the traditional aspiring working class drive to "self-improvement". And in part just chance. Visits to local museums and art galleries fitted in with the self-improvement motive. These were places that I thought I ought to visit. It was however, by chance, that I discovered that gem of an art gallery, the Barber Institute. For those who don't know it, it is to be found on the Birmingham University campus. It is a small gallery comprising a square of four rooms with works dating from the middle ages to the early twentieth century. The quality of the collection is extraordinary and can bear comparison with any small gallery in Europe. It was here that I came across the works of the French Impressionists.

I think it is not uncommon to come first to the paintings of Monet, Renoir, Sisley and others in the early development of an interest in art. I had no technical knowledge of artistic technique and no real grasp at all of the history of western painting. What first struck me was the colour and light in these paintings. Then as I read about them I saw them as radical new artists seeking to present light as they saw it, directly and with immediacy. I saw them as the counterpart of the radical movements in poetry that culminated with Eliot and others. From the Impressionists I came into contact with Gauguin, Cezanne and then Matisse. Oddly, I also developed a great liking for icon paintings from the early middle ages. I say oddly not because I think admiring icons is itself odd, I still like them, but because I have no idea how I came across them in the first place. That in a way though is an illustration of why this period was so formative and so stimulating. There were discoveries that I came across through the guidance of teachers. These in turn led onto other works of art or literature. But there were other interest, like the Impressionists and icons, that I must simply have stumbled across by chance.

Then there was the theatre. I had never been to the theatre before I went into the sixth form. It was not something my family ever did. Joyce changed all this. Dedalus had an interest in theatre. Joyce had been interested in theatre. So had Eliot. It must therefore be the right thing to be interested in. I needed to go. The obvious place in Birmingham was the Rep. In those days it was down off Hill Street. It was one of the great national repertory theatres and in its time it had some of the greatest actors of the century as part of its team including, Lawrence Olivier, Peggy Ashcroft, Ralph Richardson (all in the same year) and later Derek Jacobi. Somehow or other I ended up organising trips there. What did I see? I can't remember. That sounds dreadful but it is muddled in my memory with what I saw later when at university or in the early days of work in London. What is more important was the belief it gave me that here was another form of entertainment, of art, of cultural excitement available to me. That I had the right of entry.

I was now a poet. At least that is how I saw myself. I produced large quantities of poetry mainly under the influence of T.S. Eliot. What I captured was the fragmentation of the imagery but without any of the underlying lyricism, profundity or brilliance. So it was kind of Eliot lite. Much of it was in the mode of a dystopian vision of modern culture with a fierce denunciation of its materialism and spiritual impoverishment. It was full of images of broken columns and ruined cities. One even began with a quotation from Jeremiah's lamentation over the sacked city of Jerusalem. All terribly serious and intense. On reading one of these poems to a man I worked with later at Cadbury's on a summer vacation, I was asked in what way it was actually poetry. At the time I was too shocked by the failure of his sensibility to respond. Looking back I think he had a point.

However, the high point of my poetic career was the publication of some of my work in the school magazine and in a literary magazine edited by David Cannadine and others called, *Take Five* and winning the school debating and poetry prize for a particularly fierce diatribe on contemporary values entitled *A Modern Theology*. I can only think that the competition must have been very thin that year.

Then there was Traves the director. The young man who unwittingly produced what must have been the funniest ever production of Eugene O'Neil's *The Emperor Jones*. This would be a worthy accolade were it not for the fact that *The Emperor Jones* is a very serious play entirely devoid of humour. How did this come about?

It had been decided that there should be an inter-House drama competition. Each house would put on a one act play and a judge would be brought in to decide on the winner. The competition was to take place over two nights. Mr Butler, by this time the head of McPherson's, announced in House Assembly that this competition would take place and that in his view the right person to direct was "Our resident literary star, Peter Traves." As often in my later life, I was so flattered by praise that I did not stop to consider whether or not I had any talent or knowledge to carry out the assigned task. Going to the theatre a few times is not, I need hardly say, an adequate basis for taking on a drama production. I was not, unfortunately, aware of this fact.

The first task was to find a play. My method was simple. Simple but wrong. I went along to Hudson's bookshop in Birmingham and looked for a play that was about the right length. O'Neil's play won on this basis. In fact, I was even wrong about this as in reality it is a full length play but let that pass as it was the least of the problems this play presented.

The Emperor Jones is a very strange play. Set in a fictional Caribbean island it tells the story of the Emperor Jones, a black despot who is forced from power by a coup. He flees from his palace into the forest. In the flight he experiences visions of the middle-passage of the slave trade and gradually recedes further into his folk memory with visions of African religious rites. It ends with his death.

First challenge: this is a play with an all black cast apart from one character. Ours was an all white school. This I felt could be solved with large quantities of blacking make-up and the use of hair nets liberally sprinkled with black powder. Younger members of the school, including my brother and cousin were then coerced into the play and covered in blacking as they performed half-naked, moaning and groaning their misery in what was meant to be the bowels of a slave ship.

Second challenge: who should play the leading characters? There were two candidates for the two lead characters, Brutus Jones and his white henchman, the treacherous cockney trader, Smithers. The candidates were Mitch Price and Ron Nines. Now Brutus Jones was meant to be hugely powerful and a man of enormous charisma. Smithers is a small craven coward intimidated by Jones. Physically Ron was tall and powerful, a stalwart of the rugby team. Mitch was small and ginger haired. On that basis it should be Ron as Jones; Mitch as Smithers. The complicating problem was the accent. Mitch had talent as an actor and could also do accents. He it seemed was closer to what we all judged to be an authentic black accent. This by the way bore not resemblance whatever to any black dialect known to man or woman. Ron on the other hand could make a passable or at least occasional attempt at a cockney accent of the Dick Van Dyke variety. So on aesthetic grounds it was Mitch as Jones and Ron as Smithers. You can probably see that there were some intrinsic challenges to be overcome here that would require great skill and imagination from the director. The sight of Jones, five foot six and slight of figure attempting to tower over and intimidate Smithers, six foot and powerful of build, was not always convincing.

Third challenge: staging. This is a play with many short scenes and many changes of scenery. It is also a play that demands pace. Unfortunately as director I took it as an absolute rule that the curtains should be closed between each scene and that scenery should be on a large and elaborate scale in line with the very detailed instructions O'Neil gives in the text. It did not occur to me to use different parts of the stage to represent different places, the palace, the forest and so on. This made for an extraordinarily dislocated production with a very long break between scenes one and two as the large scale palace scenery was replaced, very noisily, behind the curtains, by the large scale forest scenery. It also did not help with regard to pace.

Fourth challenge: managing the climax. Alone in the forest Jones encounters a vision first of a crocodile and then of a witch doctor who dances before him. At this point Jones dies. Although the school was next to a large reservoir crocodiles were in short supply. This could be overcome by restricting ourselves to just the head of the croc and using papermache covered cricket bats to represent the jaws. The witch doctor was a boy in the third year. Half naked with a head-dress and blackened skin he was asked to wail and chant in a nonsense language while leaping about on stage. What should have been a nightmarish manifestation of Jones's primal horrors, was in fact a gloriously funny farce.

Final challenge: the removal of blacking from small boys' bodies. Liberal quantities of blacking cream were used on the cast. Apparently there was a cream that should be applied first. I didn't know this. A much irritated Aunt complained that it took days to get all the black stain from my young cousin Ian's face and body. I sometimes think when I see him now that he has a darker complexion than the rest of the family but I think this is just my imagination.

The scenery was commented on very positively by the judge. We were fourth. Out of four.

And so school moved towards its close. The exams were taken and like most others I looked for work over the summer. I found a job working as a chainman on a building site. The work was well paid and with overtime I made over £20 some weeks. However, this work was rudely interrupted by a very unexpected and very unwelcome letter from the headmaster. Before the exams I was a member of the school athletics team and competed in the qualifying rounds of the West Midlands' championship in the 800 metres. I had qualified from my heat for the final which was to take place later in the summer. What with the exams and the work that followed I had forgotten all about this. No one at school had informed me of the date of these games. The result was that I missed them. The head's letter was venomous. He accused me not only of letting the school down but also of a total loss of moral direction. Unless I returned immediately to school he would, he threatened, write to Birmingham City Council advising them not to give me a student grant. I returned and we met in his office.

I had always been a relatively compliant student but on this occasion I was angered by what I considered a response that was out of all proportion to the crime and by a threatened sanction that would have had dire consequences for my future. After listening to him I tried as calmly as I could to make my case. I was sorry I had missed the games but was surprised no one had thought to inform me of the date. I was also, I told him, upset that while over a period of six years or more I had turned out for the school for cross-country, cricket and athletics on weekends and in all kinds of weather, I was threatened with the effective loss of the opportunity to go to university while other boys who had never once put themselves out for the school would happily be recommended for a grant. It was one of the few occasions at that stage in my life when I was determined not to be cowed by authority. I duly served out my sentence as the only upper sixth boy in school for the remaining days and then went back to the building site as they had kindly held my job for me. In retrospect, and in the light of much greater injustices I have seen others face and triumph over, it seems a petty issue. But for young people the world is smaller and even a small injustice, a small example of power unfairly exercised, can loom large. It did for me and it soured my leaving of Five Ways.

However, despite the disappointing end to my career at Five Ways, the sixth form was a time of great change for me, of new experiences, new opportunities, a sense of life opening up. At home all was not well with ever increasing animosity between my parents as their marriage continued the long drawn-out agony of its disintegration. Academically I had moved on and culturally life was blossoming for me. In other ways life changed. I had my first real love affair and the beginning of what was to prove one of the most important of my relationships. Ultimately it did not end well, which was entirely my fault, but it was in the sixth form period a wonderful, exhilarating, loving and passionate experience.

Cross-country 1st team 1966-67 – with trophies!
Back row: Mr J. Dykes, S. Wakeling, T. Wroblewski, R. Hindley,
R. Matthews, N. Wooton, P. Traves, K. Grady, R. Forster, Mr D. Hughes
Front row: P. Crompton, J. Lakins, J. Warner, K. Humphries,
P. Carpenter, R. Mapp, P. Harrison, D. Jones.

19

Changing Birmingham

THE BIRMINGHAM of my early childhood was still predominantly the city that had grown up in the nineteenth century and that had been transformed in part by an ambitious council led by families like the Chamberlains. The dominant architecture was still very much Victorian. The population of the city was made up largely of the descendants of those people, like my ancestors, who had come in from the country during the great industrial expansion of the nineteenth century. It was still a city founded on small factories and workshops. It was overwhelmingly a white population with a strong working class and artisan basis. It was, however, a city on the crux of great change.

The problem with change as far as memory is concerned is that the eye and mind rapidly adjust to the new landscape and the new way of life to such an extent that it is hard to remember precisely what was there before. I struggle at times to recall exactly how the streets of central Birmingham were configured and connected in my early childhood or what buildings preceded some of their more modern counterparts. But this is not a history, it is a reminiscence and what I am concerned to set down is what I think I remember.

The first thing to say is that the city I recall had a different balance to its centre. The point of focus has shifted or perhaps been diffused. My memory is of a shopping centre built largely around Corporation Street and Bull Street. Perhaps because they were the heart of the shopping area, New Street and Corporation Street appeared far grander, far bigger than they seemed later. It was here that the major department stores were located, Lewis's, Grey's, Rackham's. There was also Marshall and Snelgrove's close to the inter-section of New Street and Corporation Street.

A second important area of the city was the market. The old market hall was situated on the road running down past St Martin's Church. It had suffered a direct hit in the blitz and was in the early 1950s open to the elements. The great entrance, however, remained huge and solidly classical in design with massive columns. Inside the hall were stalls and a treat for mum and me would be to buy a tiny saucer of mussels or whelks from one of these, heavily soaked by us in vinegar and lightly sprinkled with pepper. Outside the market hall was the statue commemorating Nelson's victory and death at Trafalgar and along the street running down the hill were the stalls of the outdoor market. Stall holders would call out their wares and there were some who were great performers. A little later in the 1960s I remember one stall holder who sold crockery. He would hold an array of plates, cups and saucers, held together in an elaborate arrangement and clinking as he jostled them in his arms and called out;

– Now I'm not asking £2, not thirty bob, not £1, but yours lady for fifteen bob!

On he went with banter about how he was starving himself with this offer, how the same or equivalent crockery would be at least £5 in an unnamed department store on Bull Street;

– I'm not allowed to tell you which but it starts with an 'L' and ends with an 's'.

– It's Lewis's innit, someone would say.

– You're too quick for me lady and you'll get me into trouble.

Then how as a special favour to this sharp lady in the brown coat who'd seen through his coded reference to a nameless store, he would let them go to her for thirteen bob. He was a great performer. I have no idea how much trade he did but characters like him helped create the atmosphere of a busy market.

Bull Ring circa 1950.

There was the old New Street Station with its imposing Victorian facade the huge single span roof, the largest at the time in the world or so it was claimed. It was a complex building with a number of entrances and two distinct sections linked by an enclosed foot-bridge. I rarely travelled by train as a child but I remember the excitement and the element of fear as the huge iron wheeled steam trains rolled into the station. A trip home by train was a rare treat, rare in part because Northfield station was not conveniently placed for where we lived.

New Street Station 1963.

There were also still bomb-sites in the city with isolated walls standing and huge piles of brick and rubble still to be cleared in some cases. In others the first car parks were opening.

As the fifties moved into the sixties change to the city accelerated. On Corporation Street the new Rackham's store opened with its glamorous association with the legendary Harrods. What it replaced I cannot recall. In fact Rackham's had a long and complex history in the city. William Winter Riddell and Henry Wilkinson set up a retail drapery shop in Bull Street in 1851. John Rackham and William Matthews starting in the shop as apprentices in 1863, were promoted to floor walkers and eventually took over the retail business in 1881. There were several changes of ownership and at one stage the store extended across to the North West Arcade. In 1940 it suffered a direct hit and after the war redevelopment was halted by funding problems until the company was taken over, first by Harrods in 1957, and then by House of Fraser in 1959. It was at this point that the major redevelopment began that led to it being for many decades one of, if not the, leading department store in the city. Significantly the period of Harrods' ownership was brief but left its mark in terms of the store's reputation. The older members of my family still refer to the store as Rackham's. Reputations often survive historical change, at least for a time.

Along the lower part of Corporation Street and linking onto New Street, a new shopping complex emerged with C&A and later British Home Stores. In this complex was a shop much visited by my mum, Henry's. If Rackham's and Marshal and Snelgrove's represented the upmarket image of shopping, Henry's represented the bargain basement. It seemed to me full of chaotically disordered counters of cheap and sometimes soiled goods at low prices. It was invariably packed.

The economic base of the city was changing too and this was to have its influence perhaps on its architecture. Birmingham, unlike Manchester, had grown not as the result of a single dominant industry like cotton, but as the result of the growth of small and skilled workshops. This had a profound impact not only on the economy of the city but also on its social and political make-up. However, through the 1930s the car industry grew ever more influential in the city and by the mid-1950s was employing well over

now that a new use had not been found for the lovely old library. However, the prevailing view at the time was that Victoriana was fussy, ugly and inconvenient and worst of all, not modern.

My teens were therefore a period of massive change in the appearance of the city centre. Almost every time I went into town it had changed. A familiar building had disappeared. A well known pedestrian route had been obstructed. More and more concrete was coming to dominate and more and more the late Victorian architecture that had characterised the city of my childhood was in retreat.

If the change to the appearance of the city was dramatic so was its demographic make-up. Sometime in the mid-fifties I visited Lozells Road market with grandma Traves. It was here for the first time that I saw black women, some dressed in light and colourful summer dresses in the cold English autumn. I did not realise at the time that these were the first generation of West Indian settlers. Like my in-laws, who came across from St Lucia, these men and women had been enticed to come and fill the jobs that were vacant here. Reassured by their long association with the Mother Country many of them came with a rose-tinted view of Britain and of the reception they would get. It was at this period that I noted a little sign in the door window of a house on Bristol Road South. It said;

"Room to let. No coloureds or Irish need apply."

My mother-in-law has told me of her experiences in London. Of vacancy signs being removed as they approached houses and replaced as they walked away. Of not being served in shops. Of being abused in public. I had little or no idea of this at the time. My father held pretty unpleasant views about black and Asian people and most of us were quite prepared to tell or laugh at what we would now with shame recognise as revoltingly racist jokes.

Opposite us in Fairway lived the Taylor family. Mr Taylor worked at the Longbridge. Mrs Taylor was a hardworking and meticulous mother and housekeeper. The large family of children were extremely well turned out and polite. All this was recognised by everyone who knew them. My dad, however, took strong exception to me playing with Megan Taylor who was about my age and by far the prettiest girl around. If he saw me sitting with her on their wall or talking to her he would call me in from the street. Mrs Taylor you see was black. She was not in fact part of the contemporary Windrush influx from the Caribbean. She and Mr Taylor were from Cardiff where a much older black and ethnically mixed population had been long established.

As I grew up and in the years after I left, Birmingham became an increasingly multi-cultural city. The dramatic nature of this change is only really apparent when you look back and take some kind of memory snapshot of what the city looked like in the early fifties and then contrast it with what you see today. It was then a white city, particularly in the city centre. Now the crowds you mingle with in New Street and the Bull Ring are from many parts of the world and you will hear a wide range of languages being spoken. Such a change has not been without its tensions and challenges and for some it is a change that is regretted. Not for me. I think it has made Birmingham a richer, more diverse and more vibrant city than it could ever have been and, I may be mistaken in this of course, and perhaps here I am the one wearing the rose-tinted spectacles, but I think we have made this change more effectively than most other cities I can think of. However, lack of opportunity, mixed educational outcomes and continuing poverty in some areas of the city still pose a significant threat to genuine equality.

Birmingham from the Lickey Hills 2016.

20

Villa Park

AS YOU turn off the M6 onto the Aston Expressway Villa Park looms large to your right. Impressive ground though it now is it has the appearance to me of a once stately home that has been extended by a cowboy builder without regard to the original features. True they retained, under protest as I understand it, the impressive Holte End's early twentieth century edifice, but the building as a whole has a piecemeal feel to it. I retain a nominal loyalty to Aston Villa. I say nominal because I cannot insult the real supporters who attend week in week out, season after season by attaching the same title to my own interest. I rarely go to games now. Each year I begin with very modest hopes which I then adjust downward as the season progresses. Groaning in disappointment at the score on a regular basis is not being a supporter. I recognise that fully. However, Villa Park was a significant part of my experience of growing up.

Dad was a Villa supporter in much the way that I have described my own commitment. I may have simply been following my father's preferences but there was from the start the sense that this was a football club that appealed to my sense of nostalgia, my pleasure in history. This was a club by 1959 with a great future behind it. It was still regarded as one of the aristocrats of the game but it was a noble house that had squandered most of its inheritance and where those towering teams of the late nineteenth century, winners of five league titles and two FA Cups between 1894 and 1900, must have gazed

Villa Park circa 1950.

down in profound and solemn disappointment and disapproval from their formally posed photos on the sad degeneration of the club's fortunes. Villa fans still clung to this past greatness.

However, if dad's support was luke-warm mum's Uncle Ron, my grandmother's youngest brother, was a more committed fan. Even though he lived in Lincolnshire, he regularly came down to Birmingham with his son Robert to visit family and attend games. He was the person who introduced me to Villa Park. Uncle had gone to university in the 1930s and, a very talented mathematician, he went on to become an almost legendary, deeply admired and loved teacher at Sleaford Grammar School.

My first game was long awaited. There had been a number of disappointments when my uncle was unable to come down. Finally on the last day of October 1959 I was actually going with uncle and Robert. Uncle had a car but parking near the Villa was not always easy so we met in town and took a bus to the game. Though the game started, as most games did in those days, at 3pm on a Saturday, it was as I remember a dull and slightly foggy day so that by the time we neared Villa Park the light was beginning to fade. Stepping off the bus we joined one of the tributary streams that ran towards the ground merging at Trinity Road into a flood of people that then divided either side of the Holte End Hotel. Along the roads were vendors selling programmes for the match. The closer we got the slower the pace as the backwash of the crowd from the entry gates pressed back onto us. We queued to enter with adults going through one turn-style and boys through another joining the other side in the great crush of the crowd. For that first game against Plymouth Argyle we had seats near the front in the impressive Trinity Road stand. From the crowd there was the rising fug of tobacco smoke. There was no chanting as I recall, that seems from memory to have been a feature introduced later in the 1960s. There was however the rattle. This will be familiar to older supporters but a mystery to less venerable followers of the game. A rattle was a wooden device which you twirled above your head and it made a clacking sound. Thousands of them being whirled in the air at the same time made an impressive addition to clapping or cheering. They formed part of the sound accompaniment to corners, great saves, near misses and, of course, goals. Along with a Villa scarf, I had a rattle in team colours for Christmas that year.

Villa at this stage were in the second division of the old Football League. They had won the FA cup two years before but had languished in the league and been relegated at the end of the 1958/59 season. Nevertheless crowds of over 34,000 were still commonplace at Villa Park. In the pre-Taylor inquiry days when standing in large parts of the stadium was the norm, Villa Park boasted a capacity of around 70,000 and was one of the pre-eminent grounds in the country. In those times FA Cup semi-finals were played on large neutral grounds and Villa Park held more semis than any other venue.

I remember few details of the game except that Villa won and the goals were scored by Jimmy MacEwan and Peter McParland. I remember also an incident that took place directly in front of us, a few yards away in fact. McParland was heavily tackled by a Plymouth defender. The defender seemed to come off worst and was slow to rise. As he struggled painfully to his feet McParland leaned threateningly over him and informed him in no uncertain terms that if there was any repetition of this kind of tackle he would settle the matter. The language he used to express this was the most colourful I had ever heard from an adult at that stage of my life, swearing was very rare in my family. I recall a thrill of excitement at this moment of aggression.

McParland was a gifted player, a winger who had excellent control and who could combine great skill with strength and aggression. He had scored both goals in Villa's 2-0 victory over Manchester United in the 1957 final but controversially in a legal shoulder charge of the United goalkeeper; early in the game, he had broken Woods' collarbone reducing United to ten effective players for the rest of the match. This made him the target of some abuse from oppos-

Peter McParland.

ition fans particularly as this was the gifted and popular young Busby Babes team that was emerging as a great force and which was destined for tragedy at Munich the following year.

A young player in the team that day was a man who went on to be my personal Villa hero and a figure who was hugely popular with the crowd, Gerry Hitchens. His career and life illustrate very powerfully the different world inhabited by the players of those days compared to the contemporary Premier League scene. Hitchens was born in Staffordshire and began working life as a miner playing his early football for non-league sides. He was spotted by a number of clubs but recruited in 1955 by Cardiff for £1,500. Such was the impact he made there as a centre forward that he was transferred to Villa two years later for the princely sum of £22,500. Over the next four seasons he scored 96 goals in 160 games and established himself as an England International. In 1961, much to my disappointment he was signed by Inter-Milan for what was then a mind-boggling £85,000. He played in Italy for over nine years playing for a succession of clubs and earning a great deal of affection from the Italian fans as a decisive and robust striker. On retiring from the full-time game he worked as manager of an iron works and later as the manager of a lumber merchants. He died during a non-league game at the early age of 48.

Gerry Hitchens.

No doubt Gerry Hitchens made a comfortable income from football and certainly he was a figure of glamour to fans. However, it is significant that he had to continue working after retirement. Here was an established international striker with a Europe wide reputation and yet he certainly did not end up with the kind of fabulous wealth even a relatively mundane Premier League player might expect today.

Perhaps more typical of the difference would be the mid-fielder Dave Poutney. At the time I was attending my first game at Villa Park, Dave was still playing for Shrewsbury Town. He transferred to Villa in 1963 and played several years of First Division football with them before transferring back to Shrewsbury in 1968. I came across Dave when I moved to Shropshire in 1989. He runs an excellent sports shop in Shrewsbury. Sport shops or pubs were typical of the end of career routes for good professional footballers in those days. They were of course better off than the great majority of those watching but there was not the gulf in wealth that exists today. They lived a life-style that was still recognisable to the supporter. They had good but not mansion-sized houses and drove the kind of cars that a successful manager might drive and not a Ferrari or Bugatti. Many of them like Hitchens had left school to work in industry and knew something about the lives of the working classes who paid their wages by turning out each week to support them.

I attended several more games that season including the Christmas return match against Hull. For this game we stood in the Holte End. Standing was a precarious experience for a small boy. My uncle would shepherd me through the crowd to a crush barrier. From this view point I would catch various glimpses of the game depending on the movement of the adults in front of me. Periodically the crowd would surge forward crushing me against the metal bar of the barrier. On cold days feet became bitterly cold against the concrete floor. Nevertheless the excitement and sense of involvement was always greater standing. Sometimes we stood at what was then the Witton Lane End, now the North End. In the late 1950s the terraces here were reached by an earth slope. On wet days with a big crowd moving out it could be quite a tricky business descending back down again.

The following season saw the inauguration of the League Cup. Originally proposed by Stanley Rous as a consolation competition for clubs knocked out of the FA Cup, the idea was taken up by Alan Hardaker, the Secretary of the Football League. He developed it as a means of making up for the reduced revenue clubs might expect from fewer fixtures following the reorganisation of the league. Gates were beginning to decline and clubs needed cash. The new competition was controversial however and few major clubs took it seriously. Nevertheless it was a great moment for me when Villa made it through to the final.

The final was not at Wembley in those days but was held over two legs home and away. Villa's opponents were Rotherham United who finished 15th in the old Second Division that season. Villa started as clear favourites therefore. However, as so often happens it did not turn out to be such an easy task and Villa went down 2-0 in the first leg at Millmoor. This was played late in the season, and due to a congested fixture list the second leg was held over to the following season.

Dad got tickets this time but we went along to the mid-week game with little hope of overhauling this deficit. Rotherham had been clearly the better side in the first leg. We worked our way down the Holte End terraces before kick-off and found places right at the front against the low wall behind the goal. I had a low perspective view of most of the pitch but as it turned out the position could hardly have been bettered. Rotherham held Villa for the first half and as the teams went in we had all but lost hope. Then with less than half an hour to go Alan O'Neil scored. There was now hope. Slim hope maybe, but hope nonetheless. While 2-0 looks secure, 2-1 can induce a great deal of nervousness in the defending team and such was the case with Rotherham. Only two minutes later Harry Burrows hammered the ball home from close range, the net bulging right before my eyes. The noise was fantastic. The expectation of disappointment had been transformed to one of excited anticipation. However, press as they did Villa were unable to score again in normal time. On into extra-time, a new experience for me. The first half of extra-time was goalless and the confidence of the crowd began to be tinged with nervousness. Every time Rotherham moved up field the fears of an even greater let down than a straight forward defeat reared up again. Eventually early in the second session, with just 11 minutes to go it was Peter McParland who hit the winning goal. For an eleven year old it mattered little that this was a trophy held in some contempt by the press and by major teams, this was a night of triumph, something to be held over the heretics at school who supported Birmingham City. I was to see two more Villa League Cup Finals at Wembley both of which we won and a league championship clinched despite defeat at Highbury on the last day of the season. But exciting though they were they did not match the thrill of this first trophy victory.

As with so many things related to memory, the dangers of bathing everything in the rosy glow of nostalgia is great. Let's be clear, the standard of skill shown today is far higher. The grounds are better equipped and safer. The Premier League has some of the finest players in the world and our top teams compete with the great names of Europe. Racism still exists in the game but it is less tolerated than before and there is a wealth of black talent on show now and they are less likely to be openly abused than their pioneering forebears in the 1970s. The 1950s by contrast was a period when English football was in many ways in the doldrums. Our national team had been humiliated first by Hungary and then by of all places, the USA. There were many players in the First Division who were workmanlike rather than gifted and harsh tackling was not only prevalent but actually relished and encouraged by managers and supporters. However, there were aspects of the game that seem healthier, perhaps only in retrospect but nevertheless aspects worth considering. As I have said the players inhabited a world that was broadly recognisable to the fans. Though the transfer market was active there was a clearer sense of club loyalty. Home and away fans were often mixed together and in general relations were good. It was not that much later, however, in the late 60s and 70s that the worst of football violence erupted. I first attended football matches in what appears to me now as a late flowering of the age of football's innocence.

The final point is about wit. Birmingham it seems to me excels in a unique kind of self-deprecatory humour. Three examples from Villa fans.

The first is from a slightly later period, the mid-70s when I was living in London. I got tickets for Villa's visit to Highbury. The game was dire and the main cause of this was a terrible performance by Villa and the failure of the star-studded Arsenal team to capitalise on our weakness. I was with a few other Villa fans surrounded by an increasingly frustrated and hostile Arsenal crowd. After a particularly grim passage of play one of the Villa supporters turned round and said to the Arsenal fans;

– Have yow thought, a couple of hours up the motorway an' yow could watch this kind of stuff every week?

I don't remember it being well appreciated by the Londoners.

The second was the winning final line in a dispute overheard between a Villa and Blues fan;

– We've had the Cup stolen more times than yove won it.

185

The third is in the sixties on a special match day bus heading towards Villa Park. We are overtaken by a car with Albion scarves streaming from the windows and several hands thrust out making v signs at our bus. Two old men in front of me noted this event. One turned to the other;

– D'yo see that?

– Ar.

– How many do you reckon was in that car then?

– Foive or six I reckon.

– Have yo thought then. There's them foive, Albert, Albert's mum, Sid and his brother...they must be getting nearly ten these days down the Baggies.

21

Holiday Work

IT'S HARDER for young people now in many ways. In the 60s and 70s casual work seemed easy to find and as a consequence I had a wide variety of jobs during my vacation time. This work provided not only much needed cash but also an insight into the kind of work many people do and consequently in later years it made me grateful for the opportunities I had and less tolerant towards colleagues in schools who said they sometimes felt it would be easier to work stacking shelves at Sainsbury's. My unsympathetic, but unvoiced, response was, "Try it".

By the mid-60s dad was the manager of a shop called Murdochs on Corporation Street. It sold electronic goods, records and pianos. From time to time dad would bring home piano parts for us to help renovate. The hammers had to be gently sanded down and restored to their original texture and colour. This was tedious work though in an odd sort of way satisfying. I was employed on some Saturdays and during holidays either helping in the shop or working on deliveries. I enjoyed the delivery work. I went out in a van with a man delivering washing machines, televisions, radiograms and other goods. We would stop in the morning at a cafe and have a bacon and egg sandwich and tea with several heaped spoons of sugar. The work was heavy, particularly if a washing machine was involved. What I found then and later on building sites was that the men I worked with were happy to give advice if you asked. They knew how to lift, how to manoeuvre goods through tight spaces, how to get heavy goods up or down staircases. They probably regarded me as an effete but harmless student and the fact that I asked for their help went down well though it did not protect me from either fierce teasing or practical jokes. At most working class homes we would be offered tea or coffee and sometimes biscuits or cake and an occasional tip. This was far less often the case in posher homes.

After A levels there was the prospect of months of work. Mark, Colin and I turned up at the Labour Exchange, the forerunner of Job Centres, and we were directed to a small factory out towards Nechells. The factory needed temporary workers to help with the annual stock-take. We duly turned up, were taken on and arrived the next morning for 8 to begin our work as stock-takers. We were assigned to a man who gave each of us a clipboard and who explained the work. We were to go round the various trays of screws, bolts and other widgets and count them. We were then to enter the number on the sheet, check against the previous total and record the difference. We made a start. The work as can easily be imagined was dull. We did not have to hand count all the items, we could in fact use the scales to make an assessment, but even so this was a protracted and slow process. After a couple of hours our assigned supervisor came to check how we were getting on. It was clear that he was not impressed. At the rate we were going the two week job would in fact take at least a month.

– Show us what you're doing.

We did.

He looked at us as if we were complete morons.

– Are you really, I mean really, actually counting and weighing for each tray?

– Yes, we assured him.

Again he looked at us with a mixture of contempt and pity. Then he began to explain. Management want a stock-take. As long as they get figures they will be satisfied. Our job is to provide figures and to look in the process as if we are doing the job. We do not actually have to do the job.

We still didn't catch on.

– Take a look. Then take a guess. Then write some figures down. There are proper blokes from the factory having to do this after you lot and the last thing they want is some group of toss-pot students buggering it up by actually measuring and recording.

This made the job a lot easier I have to say. It also said a lot about the relationship between workers and management in 1960s Britain. I am hoping we did not make too great a contribution to the decline of the manufacturing industry in the West Midlands.

After a few days my relief papers came through. I had a cousin who worked for Bryants and he had secured for me a job on a city centre building site. I was to be a chainman. The work comprised carrying equipment for the civil engineers and helping them in setting down grid lines and markers of height. When work was slack for the engineers I would be put on to general labouring. There were several students on the site at the time. We were generally regarded as a waste of space by most of the labourers. None of us had done hard physical work of the kind demanded on site. For the first few weeks my hands bled by day, healed each night and opened up again the following morning. Gradually they calloused and the bleeding stopped. We were also regarded as fair game for practical jokes, many of which were based on our general feebleness compared to the labourers. One day I was sent down to get a bucket of concrete by the engineers from a lorry that was pouring on site. I would then use this to make blocks that would be tested for strength. I took the oversized bucket along to the lorry and handed it over to a mountain of a man who was standing by the shute. He held the bucket under the flow as it filled up. From the apparent strain he showed it could have been filling with feathers. When it was full he handed it over. Now I had never carried a large bucket of concrete. I had in my head a weight like a bucket of water. Concrete, as I was soon to discover, is heavy. Very heavy. As I took the bucket from him I felt the tremendous strain on my arms, shoulders and neck. Every muscle, every ligament felt as if it were about to tear. I could see him suppressing laughter and felt the eyes of several other labourers. I had a walk of several hundred yards with this bucket. I was to be watched at every stage. I knew that I could not stop, could not change hands, could not show any sign that this was anything other than mild exercise for me. I succeeded though my muscles ached for days.

I got to know the labourers. They were a decent lot when you spent time talking to them and they were helpful and once I had been there a while they acted to protect me from the worst and heaviest of the work. One afternoon I spent several hours working alongside a man who got to talking at length about his childhood in rural Ireland and his early experiences as an immigrant in England. He asked me what I planned to do with my life and made it clear that I should take my chances not to end up in the kind of work he was doing now. For whatever reason, perhaps he thought me vulnerable or innocent, he took to me and was serious in his desire that I should make the most of my education. One of the linguistic skills the labourers had was the ability to insert one form or another of the words "f**k" or "f***ing", not only into pretty well every sentence but even into the middle of long words, as in "For f**ks sake, he's unre-f***ing-liable, that's what he f***ing well is."

The work involved a great deal of scrambling around on scaffolding and shuttering, often several storeys up. I am not naturally good at heights but I handled this pretty well. Not of course as well as the experienced labourers. However, there was one day when I did manage to win their respect. A deep shaft was being bored. I seem to remember it was related to a lift. It was less than three feet in diameter and about seventy feet deep. The engineers needed to check the alignment of the hole. To do this they needed someone to go down the hole. I volunteered. I stood on the hook of a crane and was lowered down. As I went deeper the space seemed to close around me and the smell of the moist, sandy earth was all pervasive. I could hear the scraping of the giant earth movers on a lower level of the site. The hole at the opening narrowed to a tiny point of light. I suppressed, as best I could, all thought of what would happen if the shaft collapsed on me. I did the job and was lifted back out. A number of labourers expressed the fact that they would not have "f***ing done that for twice the weekly bonus." Others made the simple statement that I must be "one of them brainy f***ing idiots."

There was plenty of over-time available and as I was not paying taxes I saved a good amount of money that summer. I returned to work on building sites the following summer. I have a healthy respect for the men, and now women, who work in construction. It's hard, and I would fall asleep each evening within minutes of boarding the 63 bus from Navigation Street. It's hard and it's skilled and I knew that though I had done it for three months I had not done it as well as the real labourers and never could. Nor could I have done it for a working life. Another reason to be grateful for the opportunities education offered me.

My mum worked at Cadbury's and she got me employment there two summers in a row. The first year was a plum job in the laboratories testing wrapping paper and chocolate. The second year however, was the harder but more lucrative night work on the belt. I was part of a team packing marshmallows. All night as the boxes moved along the belt I packed in three pink, three white, three pink. The boredom of the task was alleviated by the humour on the belt. Among the team were twins who had been apprentices at Villa and they told great stories about Tommy Docherty and his uncompromising expectations about the ferocity of tackling he demanded and his vivid use of swear words that might have made even my co-workers on the building sites blush. We also found that we fell in with a desire to break production records and roundly cursed anyone who slowed the work down. Among my few claims to fame is that I was a pretty nifty marshmallow packer and certainly kept pace with the best.

The rule at Cadbury's was that taking any produce out of the factory was a sackable offence but while in work you could eat as much chocolate as you liked. The received wisdom was that you quickly got sated with chocolate and didn't bother after a while. We were packing marshmallows and I don't like them, but behind us was a belt packing a large selection box for Christmas sale. I have to say I did not get sated in the time I worked there.

Cadbury's had a reputation as a good employer. While there I got a chance to play for one of their cricket teams. Food in the canteen was excellent and I had no problem eating my main daily meal just after one in the morning. There was also the weekly film. This I think prepared me for avant garde movies and post-modernist literature with their tendencies to dislocate the narrative. Meal break times were staggered over several hours for the different teams. The film would start on the Monday to coincide with the earliest of the team breaks. Each team would get to see between twenty or thirty minutes of the film each night. For the team on first break they would see the film sequentially from its beginning on Monday to its conclusion on Thursday. However, for our team it meant starting on Monday with a film that was already over half way through, finishing it on Tuesday and then watching the first half on Wednesday and Thursday. You became very adept at piecing together the narrative from a very different perspective than the conventional linear viewing. There are several great films from the time including the original *Alfie* that I viewed in this way. It gave me a very different and sometimes rather odd perspective on them.

Towards the end of my time at university my girlfriend's father got me a summer job at Dollond and Aitchison, spectacle makers. I had the job of "springer in". A box would come down the belt with frames and lenses. The job of the springer in was to heat the frames in a small oven and then when the plastic had become sufficiently pliable "spring" the lenses in. You had to judge the right length of time in the oven. Too brief a time and the lenses would not go in. Too long a time and the frames would be reduced to a floppy mess. I tended to stray towards the too long model of timing and was taken to task for the waste of expensive frames. Whatever my short-comings as a springer in, I survived the whole summer so either I have been harsh in my self-judgment, or perhaps, their supervision was slack.

A feature of factory work that I noted was its impact on time. Time appears to be a constant. Each hour is filled with the same number of minutes and each minute with a constant number of seconds. A well regulated clock or watch moves through the record of these seconds, minutes and hours at the same pace. It maintains this pace whatever you are engaged in. That at least is the common-sense view though it may of course not accord with more advanced theories of time and space. Whatever the common sense view says, it is wrong. Try observing the movement of time when you are engaged in really dull, tedious work. You do everything you can not to watch the clock. You look 11-47. You look away and concentrate on everything but the movement of time. You focus on your work. You run through what you intend to do that night, that weekend. You speculate about the lives of fellow workers. After the passage of at least an hour you look up at the clock 11-55. Time moved slower in these jobs and I state this as an indisputable fact.

A second feature was the social hierarchy in action. Management were superior to shop floor workers. Managers above a certain level ate separately in their own dining room. They had reserved parking spaces. They wore suits. The best of them were respected as decent blokes (they were pretty well all "blokes" at most of the factories) but they were still distinct. The senior managers were seen as an entirely different species living an entirely different life. What was more surprising was the extent to which the lowest paid clerical workers tended to look down on shop floor workers. Despite the skills of many of the factory hands, and their higher pay, the clerical staff treated them with an air of superiority and associated themselves with their managerial bosses.

My favourite job was the Christmas post. I genuinely enjoyed this. Every year the post office took on thousands of casual workers to help sort and deliver the Christmas post. I worked at a number of post-offices over a six year period. It meant an early start getting up in the cold and dark to go in to sort out your own mail for delivery. I never minded this. You worked with a post man or woman who delegated part of the round to you. There must be unpleasant and mean spirited post men and women, it's just, perhaps, that I never met one. They were unfailingly helpful in guiding you to do the job quickly and accurately. They took pride in what they did and in the delivery of a daily service. The team spirit was great and the workplace good humoured and friendly. You sorted the mail so that it ran efficiently in the order as it would be delivered. This might mean that mail for a close or crescent would be set in the middle of a run along a road. Oddities in numbering would be taken into account. The post man or woman would know the most time-effective way to do the round. All you had to do was take note and sort and bundle accordingly packing your bag so that it followed this order. It was also a job where time never dragged and where if you worked quickly you finished early. My grandfather had been a postal worker for over fifty years and I came to this job with a positive image of the postal service. It did not disappoint me.

Casual vacation work meant being able to go away on holiday. It meant starting each academic year with a fund that would supplement the grant. It meant a greater degree of financial independence. It also meant, as I hinted earlier, that I gained some insight into the fact that many people who did not have the luck I had in education, did hard and often tedious work and sometimes low paid jobs for their whole working life. This experience made me grateful and meant I was less likely to take for granted the advantages and opportunities I had been handed. Finally, it gave me a respect for people who had skills I never gained. Skills that involved physical strength, endurance, fine motor skills and judgement. I recognised in them aptitudes I never really acquired and which, fortunately for me, were never demanded in the work I went on to do.

22

The Breakdown of a Marriage

"All happy families are alike but an unhappy family is unhappy after its own fashion."
– Tolstoy, Anna Karenin

Mum and Dad in the wedding car 1949.

INE WAS in many ways, and compared to so many others, a fortunate childhood. Though we were not wealthy we never went hungry. My parents were very supportive of my education and took great pains to provide extras like an annual holiday. I was part of a close extended family, particularly on my mother's side, and was the recipient of great affection, some would say favouritism, from my grandparents. School was generally a positive experience and I had a good circle of friends. I enjoyed sport and had a modicum of talent for some of it. This chapter then is not the outpouring of an abused child or the painful expression of prolonged misery. Nor can I claim that my life has been ruined or even greatly marred by what happened to my family, though it may have had its own subtle impact on my personality. It is rather an attempt to give form to what many children experience, the breakdown of relations between the two people they most love, their mother and their father. It is a commonplace experience perhaps, but for each child it is unique and, in most cases, it is one that is bitter. Each case has its own particular and peculiar features, its own emotional pallet.

Divorce was far less common in my childhood and for ordinary people still carried a heavy social stigma. This almost certainly meant that many ill-matched couples stayed together in mutual unhappiness. One of the features of my parents' marital breakdown was the fact that it took place in a period extending over more than a decade and it was this prolongation of the process that gave it its own specific shading, its own distinctive character. In terms of a conflict this was a war of attrition fought until the two exhausted sides could take no more and surrendered to the inevitable. Nor was

Mum and dad 1949 Lickey Church, Rednal, Birmingham.

it a conflict that ended with a peace treaty that led over time to reconciliation, the bitterness lingered, and if anything deepened, to the end of both their lives.

I was about eleven when it all became real for me. One day as I was helping mum hang out the washing she suddenly announced that my father was having an affair with someone he worked with. No preparatory comments, no sitting me down to take on this bombshell of a fact, just straight out with it. My response was simple and categorical denial. Not my dad. This simply could not be true. Mum insisted. She named the woman. Gave some details of the evidence, lipstick on shirts that kind of thing. I refused to be convinced. This could not be true.

My anger was directed at her. In many ways that continued to be the pattern of my behaviour for much of the next decade; anger not at my father for his unfaithfulness and his deceit, but at mum for telling me, for confiding in me, for embarrassing me. This was not a very noble or compassionate way to behave. Mum was after all the victim in all this. My only excuse is that I was a child and then an adolescent. I was not strong enough to lend mum my support and I certainly was not strong enough to take on my dad. I simply wanted it to go away. Ideally it would go away by not being true. Once that became impossible, once the evidence was too strong even for me to overlook, it would go away I hoped, by being ignored by not being acknowledged.

An unhappy marriage must be unbearable for the adults concerned and it is a good and humane thing that they can get out of this situation now. Often the ending of an unhappy relationship is clearly in the best interest of the children and adults may have a responsibility to take this decision on their behalf. However, my personal experience, and my later experience from working with young people, is that many children involved would prefer any continuing relationship between their parents to their separation. They may be mistaken in this desire, they often are. Separation may lead to a more secure long-term life for the child, but this is not how they are likely to feel at the time. This is not presented in any way as an argument against separation or divorce, far from it, but simply as a genuinely held belief based on my observations about how children often experience the process of the breakdown of parental relationships.

Dad was a highly intelligent and able man who did well given the fact that he left school at 14 with no qualifications and went to work the following week in a factory. By hard work and innate ability he worked his way up to a good managerial position in retail over the years but along the way he must have noted the fact that less able men from more advantaged backgrounds or with better formal qualifications were promoted ahead of him. From what I can piece together he had very limited experience of women before meeting and falling in love with my mother.

Mum was from a loving family and she was the object of affection not only from her parents but from the extended Vincent and Underhill families. To her death mum remained a much loved figure among her sisters, aunts, uncles, nieces, nephews and cousins. She had never encountered betrayal or harshness and as a result she had no inbuilt resilience to deal with what was to happen to her marriage. Before marriage mum had had a number of pretty innocent relationships with men, including at least one with a GI officer. She was a confident, intelligent and beautiful young woman when she fell deeply in love with and then married my father.

From early childhood I remember that dad's moods could dominate the household. He was not violent or abusive in any way but when he was in a dark mood we all had to take great care to steer clear of him and not in any way upset him. Mum was often openly worried about what mood he would be in when he returned home from work. Dad was a very good looking man and I suspect this was not something that he had been particularly aware of when he was young, before he married. It was all too evident from his later behaviour that once he became aware of his attractiveness to women he made use of it. I do not want to suggest for one moment that my father was a philanderer. He was I think flattered by the attentions he received and frustrated by his career and to some extent by his life. This of course is all speculation on my part. I never discussed the matter with my dad; that would have been unthinkable to me and to him. Whatever the cause he was having the first of a number of affairs. Mum had found out about it and she had told me. That was the start.

The tension between my parents rapidly increased and there was little attempt, particularly on mum's side, to disguise it. Dad was the guilty party. He lied to my mother and he later lied to me. Cruelly he would suggest it was part of delusional behaviour by mum. However, from my point of view it was an invisible guilt, a guilt that could be ignored so that life could carry on as usual. As long as no one spoke openly about it at least the veneer of normality could be retained. Dad had no intention of talking about it in front of me. Mum on the other hand had no intention whatsoever of letting matters stay quiet. Hence it was mum who unfairly attracted most of my anger and irritation.

I suspect that there were attempts at peace, at trying to see if they could make a go of it. Mum's problem was that her love and her trust had been absolute and once betrayed they were betrayed absolutely. Her model for a relationship was her parents' marriage: complete mutual affection, complete loyalty and complete trust. She could envisage no other model. She could not therefore manage the lowering of expectations that were required for a compromise; for the rebuilding of a relationship on new and more realistic terms. What I cannot know is whether dad had any real intentions of remaining faithful, whether there was therefore any real prospect of reconciliation. What I observed was mum's behaviour.

Mum's inability to let matters lie would come out in sudden and unexpected lines of questioning and conversation. At tea while the conversation wandered from trivial subject to trivial subject she would suddenly take things in a new direction. I soon learned to recognise and dread the signs. On one occasion when I had a friend round I remember her saying from out of nowhere;

– Do you like the houses in (such and such) a street, Reg?

From dad's response I knew that this was not an innocent inquiry.

– Not particularly.

(Pause)

– Really? That's interesting.

– Why interesting? Asked my father with an increased level of irritation.

– Nothing really. It doesn't matter. I just wondered.

A brief and awkward silence then;

– So you're not especially interested in those houses in (such and such) a street then Reg?

– Should I be then?

– No, just odd really.

– What's odd? What are you on about Beryl?

– Nothing.

Another even more awkward silence and a desperate desire on my part to get my friend away from the table as fast as possible.

– Just odd really... odd that your car has been seen parked outside a house there on a number of occasions after work. Don't you have a little friend there?

Dad, I recall then threw down his knife and fork and stormed out of the house.

I am ashamed to say that my feelings about this were not pity for my mum but acute embarrassment. The explanation to my friend that my mum and dad were mad, was unlikely to have convinced him.

The other type of scenes, often far more dramatic took place after my brother and I had gone to bed. I hear from the bedroom the rising murmur of voices below and the clear signals of a brewing storm. I creep down onto the stairs to listen in as best I can, horrified and fascinated at the same time by the ferocity of the accusations and counter-attacks. Dad's line as always is to question mum's sanity over these claims. The argument erupts into full-scale yelling matches spilling over into the street as dad makes his exit. By sixteen I had enough of a social life to escape for large parts of the time and I had left home by 18. For Richard who was five years younger the strain and the pain must have been so much greater. Eventually they did separate but it had taken a long time and a heavy toll.

Dad lived a life in which he denied the relationship he later established with another woman. She obviously moved out whenever I visited but the absurdity of the pretence was fantastic, her clothes and cosmetics were around the house. I had no intentions of pursuing this matter. Both of us left the obvious unsaid, unacknowledged. He finally introduced her as he was dying of cancer and married her a week or so before his death.

For mum the betrayal continued to eat away at her up to and past dad's death. She had a wonderful capacity for friendship that she extended to her relatives and friends who adored her. She was the most gifted and loving of grandmothers. However, though we got on well and though there was so much to admire and love about her, the betrayal loomed large in conversation and it embittered her at times. She had wanted my support through my teens and I had not been able to give it. I regret that and perhaps a better or stronger young person might have given it. My excuse is that I was just an ordinary flawed adolescent with all the anxieties and egocentricity common with developing young men. Perhaps more simply my moral courage was tested and found wanting.

23

Leaving Birmingham

M Y PARENTS moved out of Birmingham to Halesowen in 1967. I was still in the sixth form and spent much of my time at my grandmother's in Rednal. The fact that my girlfriend, Christine, lived in nearby Rubery may have added to my desire to stay within the city boundaries. I worked that summer on a building site in the city centre and spent many evenings and every weekend out in clubs and pubs. However, my departure from Birmingham had merely been delayed. In the autumn of 1968 with a crop of good A level results I was off to Swansea University. The night before I left, Christine and I went to the Rainbow Club for a farewell with friends like Mark. It was a night of slightly drunken sentimentality with dances to old Motown classics and in particular the Rainbow anthem, *This Old Heart of Mine*. The following day mum and dad drove me down to Swansea. I would not return to live in Birmingham for 42 years.

I did not break my ties all at once or entirely. For a while my parents continued to live in Halesowen and Christine lived in Rubery. As a consequence, I returned for some weekends and all holidays for my first two years in Swansea. My parents then began a series of moves, first to Scotland and then to Bristol and on to Trowbridge in Wiltshire before finally splitting. Christine joined me in Swansea in 1970. My final two years of research led to summer work in Cambridge. My return trips to Birmingham became more rare. After five years at Swansea I moved to London, first to study at the Institute of Education and then to teaching and advisory work. Over the next 16 years I lived in various parts of London before moving to Shropshire where I have lived for over 25 years.

As a student and when living in London, I often found myself fiercely defending the city against those whose only impression of it was the unflattering view of urban sprawl and industrial decay as they crawled past in traffic jams on the M6. As part of my case: I cited its nineteenth history as a pioneer of urban governance; the fact that it undertook the public ownership of water and gas; that it instituted the first programmes of slum clearance; that it was a city of a "thousand trades"; and that it was the centre of the Pre-Raphaelite movement. I was outraged by the numerous surveys that placed the Brummie accent as the least attractive in the country, I still am, and I ranted about the prejudice against the great new Victorian cities that underlay these views. I secretly mourned the passing of the Victorian city I had grown up in and deplored the ugliness of much of the development of the 1970s, but remained publicly loyal to what I always regarded as my home city.

I still had family and friends in Birmingham and visited them from time to time but I had no anchor in the city anymore. My visits were spasmodic and increasingly rare as the years went on. My link to the city became one rooted in memory, in sentiment. My accent has faded though as soon as people know I come from Birmingham they say they can pick up trace elements in my voice, in the stress I give to certain vowels and consonants. My three children have no substantial connection to the city, although the youngest of them is a Villa supporter. All three of them like the city however, and when we had a flat there for two years they loved coming to stay and taking advantage of what the city can offer. In the long continuing rivalry with Manchester that has its roots in the nineteenth century, my wife and sons have come down firmly against the northern pretender to the claim of second city. I do not believe that this is only out of loyalty to me, but rather it is a validation of their good taste and sound judgement.

I have lived therefore a significantly greater part of my life away from Birmingham than in it. And yet, if asked, "Where are you from?" I will invariably answer, "Birmingham". I was not born there. I do not live there and I left it over forty years ago, but I feel myself to have my roots in this unfashionable but great city.

24

The Return to Birmingham

I LIVED and worked in London for sixteen years but in 1989 we moved to Shropshire and settled in the village of Pontesbury and quickly grew to love this beautiful county. Birmingham was now our nearest city. We began to make full use of it. We went there to visit relatives. We shopped there. Saw films there. Ate out there. Went to concerts and to the theatre. Wandered its streets and canals. To my delight, my wife, Merle, grew to like Birmingham more and more. Above all she appreciated the friendliness of the city which she contrasted with London. In 2010 Merle took a job in a school in Nechells, an inner and deprived

Pontesford Hill, Shropshire.

area of Birmingham. I was working at the time in Staffordshire but was coming towards retirement. We took the decision to rent a flat in Birmingham and to live there mid-week and return to Shropshire at weekends. We found one on St Paul's Square.

We moved in and for the first few months I commuted to Stafford. For a few months more I was seconded to a post based in

205

the Government Office of the West Midlands and was located in a building facing St Phillip's. We were living, and I was working, within a few hundred yards of where one of my ancestors lived on first arriving in Birmingham, in what had then been a notorious slum in Fleet Street. These were the people who had moved to the city from rural Warwickshire looking for a better life in the mid-nineteenth century. He made that better life for his family becoming a master jeweller, the first of several of my antecedents who worked in the jewellery trade. Now here we were plying our very different trades in the city.

In the summer of 2010 I retired from full time work but continued to take work as a consultant, working often in London. I had however, more time than ever before to enjoy my return to Birmingham. Merle's work was hard in a school facing problems but nevertheless we had time to take advantage of all that Birmingham has to offer. We went to more classical concerts, several in the wonderfully refurbished Town Hall. We rediscovered England's oldest continuously operating cinema, The Electric in Hill Street. We found the wonderful restaurant Simpsons out near the Botanical Gardens. We hardly missed an exhibition at the galleries and we ate out at least twice a week, often in St Paul's Square or the surrounding area. We went on long walks around the streets and along the canals. In short, we made the most of the city. Our sons and friends made use of the flat, especially at weekends and holidays and many of them came to appreciate Birmingham. This appreciation was always a source of greatest satisfaction if the person came from London.

Sadly the return was relatively short-lived. Merle contracted lymphoma, a form of blood cancer, and after extensive and successful treatment, she retired and we returned to Shropshire. For a while we kept on the St Paul's flat but ultimately had to face the fact that it was an expensive luxury and had to let it go.

The return however was hugely important. It reconnected me with my city in a more profound way than I could have imagined. I had retained a latent affection for the city and enjoyed our visits there from Shropshire, what the return did was to enliven that affection, give form to it. On days I was not working I revelled in simply wandering the city centre and the back-streets. I loved hearing the accent all around me and hearing it spoken by people of so many different cultural and ethnic backgrounds. The accent seemed a symbol of the fact that Muslim, Christian or Hindu and of whatever ethnic origin, these people are all Brummies, part of a new and rejuvenated city. I realised more fully than ever before that I felt at home with this accent; felt at home in this city. I don't live there now but we visit a great deal. Periodically we take any excuse to book a night or two in a hotel or apartment in the city and we make the most of our time there.

So over the time I have known the city, what has changed and what has remained constant? The ethnographic profile of the city has, as I have said earlier, changed out of all recognition. Birmingham is now a multi-cultural, multi-ethnic and multi-faith city. All the better for it in my opinion. Some of the buildings of my childhood have gone. Some of the best of the old Victorian city was torn down; for the worse in my opinion – but you might expect such a view from a grumpy old man. There are still areas of great deprivation where too many people feel let down and disconnected from the growing affluence of the majority. Cuts in public spending threaten civic provision and much that is positive about urban life. However, the city has made a great recovery from the worst excesses of poor planning. There is now a vibrant cultural centre with two of the finest music venues in Britain, the Town Hall and the Symphony Hall, the wonderful art gallery and museum, the repertory theatre and now the magnificent new public library, all within a few hundred yards of each other. The canal areas that were in sad decline for so long, have been made into a real feature of the city centre. It is a brighter and more vibrant city and though for a while I think it lost its self-confidence, this seems to have come back.

Brummies still exercise their long established dour and self-deprecatory sense of humour about themselves and their city. On a radio programme about Birmingham the interviewer pointed out the long running line that Birmingham has more miles of canal than Venice. After a pause for thought the Brummie answered;

– Yeah, that's true …but somehow people seem to prefer going to Venice.

No over-confident cockney or boastful Mancunian would come out with such a line. But beneath the self-critical humour there is a pride, a pride that allows us to poke fun at ourselves and our city. I no longer live in Birmingham and have lived away for most of my life, but I am at heart a Brummie and I have been profoundly shaped by its people and by the culture and the feel of this remarkable city.